Mary Madigan is a spiritual psychic reader, healer, and Reiki Master. After being called to service, Mary found a deep connection with Archangel Michael's well in Lixnaw, County Kerry.

When Mary was a child, her amazing intuitive gift was well recognised by family. A traditional Irish family, with deep religious beliefs and convictions common with the culture of the time.

A natural intuitive healer, Mary's gifts and understanding were strengthened by a personal healing journey. Divinely guided and challenged by life, Mary embarked on a voyage of self-discovery, a journey that will continue for the rest of her days. This journey has taught Mary just how controlled our lives can be by our past.

Through an incredible connection with Our Lady and Padre Pio, there has been a newfound direction as a healer; psychic and spiritual gifts have expanded and developed. Over the past seven years, visiting both Padre Pio's resting place at San Giovanni Rotunda and Medjugorje, the area near Bosnia and Herzegovina known for apparitions of Our Lady since 1981, has enhanced the depth of her spiritual affiliation.

Mary met the love of her life in January 1980, when Johnny

Logan won the Eurovision Song Contest. They got married in August 1987, the Marian year in Ireland. Their firstbornwas Michael. He has angel wings. Second-born, James came along; he is now in his thirties. Their third child, Lizzy, joined Michael in heaven. Then, their dear daughter Nora came along. Recently, Mary has received more incredible joy with two stunning grandchildren.

Mary lives in a small village in County Kerry, Ireland. She had worked in a local shop for a while, then a pharmacy, then had an amazing time with bar work, which she ran single-handedly; it was known as 'bikers bar'. Mary has been fortunate enough to have travelled to many places around the globe, including a stay in Boston, USA, visiting Ground Zero whilst in New York and also staying in Vermont, which she adores. Additionally, Germany and Poland for extensive visits, including emotionally charged concentration camps such as Warsaw, Neuengamme, Auschwitz, Dachau, Treblinka.

Mary imagines people have always found her strange, but the sixth sense has been a major part of her for as long as she can remember. Sometimes, people say they have visions of Mary standing over them in bed whilst Mary is placing her hands on them. Others have reported seeing Mary in spirit at the foot of their stairs. Mary often feels things about people before they even come to her for a reading or consultation, allowing her to prepare through this ability. It is these extraordinary events, possibly strange, that certainly illustrate spirituality and, of course, something very different from others in this world.

It is a great honour for me to dedicate this book to:
My dad, Joe (Joseph) Madigan and Dad's mother, Nan—
Katie (Catherine) Madigan.

I will be forever grateful for the roles they played in my life.
Bless them.

Mary Madigan

BENEATH THE MOUNTAIN

The True Story of a Psychic and Spiritual Healer

AUSTIN MACAULEY PUBLISHERS®
LONDON • CAMBRIDGE • NEW YORK • SHARJAH

All of the events in this memoir are true to the best of author's memory. The views expressed in this memoir are solely those of the author.

A CIP catalogue record for this title is available from the British Library.

ISBN 9781035874170 (Paperback)
ISBN 9781035874187 (Hardback)
ISBN 9781035874200 (ePub e-book)
ISBN 9781035874194 (Audiobook)

www.austinmacauley.com

First Published 2025
Austin Macauley Publishers Ltd®
1 Canada Square
Canary Wharf
London
E14 5AA

To my husband, Tony, I wish to thank him for all the love and support he has given me throughout my life. We have gone through difficult times together and have weathered many storms. He has a wonderfully caring spirit, and I am proud of him and really happy to have shared my life and love with him.

To my four children, I am grateful for you all. James and Nora, I wish I could have protected both of you from the pain you felt at birth and growing up and the abandonment that, at times, you must have experienced. You are shining lights who have given me so much, and you were absolutely worth it. To my little angels, Michael and Lizzie, your time here on earth was so brief, but I cherish the knowledge that you are both happy in heaven, and I know that eventually, one day, we will all be together as one complete celestial family.

Finally, I want to acknowledge the woman who gave birth to me, my mum, Nora (née O'Sullivan) Madigan. Thank God, at eighty-three, she is still here today and as determined as ever.

Chapter 1
Early Days

I weighed in at just under seven pounds on 11th October 1962. My place of birth was old St Catherine's Hospital in Tralee, a former workhouse that has since closed down and been replaced by Kerry General Hospital. By all accounts, I was a healthy baby with a strong pair of lungs on me. Bright and bouncy with blue eyes and a ready smile, I was the second daughter to Joe and Noreen Madigan, who owned a small farm in Ballybunion. This picturesque village is in the heart of County Kerry.

It was common at the time for paperwork to be a bit sketchy at best in hospitals, so when it was found out the medical records surrounding my birth had gone missing, there wasn't much fuss made about it. The main priority was that both mother and baby were safe and well. My name was not initially Mary. It was Catherine, and no, not after the hospital I was born in but after a nun who worked in the hospital and who took care of my mum while she was there.

Mum took a liking to this nun because the sister was very kind and warm-hearted. Would you believe Catherine was also my paternal grandmother's name? With the amount of

Catherines surrounding me, it was as if I really had no choice but to be called by that name.

My mum was deeply affected when Sister Catherine expressed regret that she never had a daughter herself. She said she would have loved to have a child, particularly a girl. It would have been such a gift. Back then, a lot of Catholic families were large, and it was often strongly suggested to a particular son or daughter that they should enter religious life. It was considered a great honour to have a nun or priest in the family, but in truth, the young man or woman usually had little or no choice in the matter. Religious life offered a safe and secure future and, with a bit of luck, bonus points when it came to the time for Mum and Dad to go home and meet their creator.

Being well aware of these traditions, Mum felt it would be lovely to honour this nun by naming me after her. She also gave me Sister Catherine's second and third names, which were Brenda and Mary. So I got christened Catherine Brenda Mary Madigan.

However, there was a problem. Because my grandmother's name was Catherine, it was agreed it would cause confusion in the family if I was called the same name, so they decided to christen me Catherine and call me Kathleen instead. How much more Irish can you get?

To be honest, it was funny to have so many names. I wore them like hats, and over the years, I have switched them around when I felt like it. It confused people back then and still does to this day. As a child, I often played pretend and talked to myself using my different names and acted like I was different people. It was great fun.

When Mum and Dad took me home from the hospital, it was to a little Irish cottage dwelling under the gaze of the mountain, Cnoc An Óir, only three miles from Ballybunion's beautiful beach. It was a place I loved from the start. It was my *Tir na nÓg*—the land of my youth.

Today, it is still very much part of my own sacred space, a place where I really belong.

When my parents married, they came to live with Nan, my dad's mother and Tady, her brother and my grand-uncle, in this typical traditional cottage. Our home was a single-storey house, the front of which consisted of a sash window beside a door that was divided into two halves. An old galvanised tin roof sat overhead. Inside were a large room that served as a living space, kitchen and two bedrooms.

Often the top half of the door was left open as Nan and Tady liked to watch the world go by. Now and again, I would wonder what they were watching because there wasn't a lot of disruption or activity happening outside our secluded home. Maybe they just watched the peace and marvelled at nature while breathing in the fresh country air with all its beautiful aromas wafting from the fields and the plants and flowers nearby. This would only happen on good days when they were best pals because, on bad days, they were sworn enemies and would stay apart from each other.

It was great during the summer, as the light of the day and the fresh scents and sounds of life were brought into the little cottage by just swinging open the doors. The gurgling of the river nearby added to the music of the natural world that came into our home. In poor weather, the door would be shut, and the rain could be heard dancing on the tin roof and sounding like a little waterfall as it rolled down the gutters to the drains, while the winds whistled around the house and the trees swayed backwards and forwards.

Since the only two bedrooms in the cottage belonged to Nan and Tady, Mum and Dad had to sleep on a mattress in the main room. When I arrived in the house, I was first put in a cot at night-time, and when I grew older, I slept with Mum, Dad and my big sister on the mattress. I felt completely safe and comfortable sleeping with my family in this way. Every morning, the bedclothes would be folded up and put in one of the bedrooms, along with the mattress, making way for a hearty breakfast of porridge with griddle bread smeared in butter and gooseberry jam, yum. Then the new day would begin.

I know by today's standards the main living area in the cottage would be considered very cramped, but back then, it was not so unusual to have large families in small houses, and though space was tight so were families.

They say home is where the heart is; well, Kerry is home to me. From where we lived, at times, I could smell the clean, salty scent of the sea in the air. There was also a little river flowing by the house where I, as a little child, would while away the hours in peace and solitude. There I was held in the arms of Mother Nature, and I felt I lived in God's beautiful garden which He created especially for my family and me. I loved the peace and joy that the natural world gave me.

I have fond memories of these times. I remember the fresh smell of Nan's baking. I loved all her bread and tarts, especially the griddle cakes that I was very partial to, particularly when they were smothered in the home-churned creamy butter, which my mother used to make. My mouth waters when I think about them now, and they bring back a feeling of homeliness in my heart. Mum and Nan used to knit cardigans and jumpers for my sister and me, and Nan, who was a skilled seamstress, created beautiful dresses for us on her Singer sewing machine.

Mum tried to make me look pretty, but all I wanted to do was wear my trousers, wellies and jumper because I was happiest playing out in the fields and going on my rambles, where I was free to roll in the grass or stamp in the puddles.

'It's not worth fighting over,' my mum said resignedly over my choice of clothes.

I'd go out tidy enough, but Mum could tell where I was by the way I looked and smelled when I came home. Now and again, she tied up my long hair in ponytails or pigtails. No doubt she hoped she would get a positive reaction from me and that her daughter might start acting more like the pretty little girl she was. But it didn't work. It sure didn't help when my brother joked that I had pig's tails on my head. I recall snarling at him and walking off in a huff.

One day, Mum put a green ribbon on my hair for St Patrick's Day. *Yuck*, I thought, when I looked at myself in the mirror. I really didn't like looking like a sweet little Irish cailín. You could keep all your frills and shamrocks as far as I was concerned. They would be far too fussy for me.

My family would say as I grew up I was a bright, chatty and funny little girl. I learned to walk and talk quite quickly and was always up for an adventure. The stories I relate to in my early childhood are the tales I was told by my family in later years. I was brim-full of curiosity, and there were many stories told of the escapades of daredevil Kathleen Catherine Mary Brenda, and with four names of course, I had to get up to four times the mischief!

Saturday night was bath night. The fire was stoked up, and all of us got washed in one bath of water. My nan had a sense of humour, and she would say, 'Can I hold your Palmolive? Not on your Lifebuoy.' They were the brands of the two soaps sold in the shops at the time.

The bath would be placed at the roaring fire, and everyone would wash, one after the other. We all wanted the first wash because the water was clean then. It was hard work to have a bath in those days as all our water had to be drawn from the well up the road. I used to hate doing it because the well was open and deep and sometimes smelly from the animals. I can almost hear the splish-splash of the water in the tin bucket as I carried my fair share back to the house.

On top of that, there was always the risk of tripping and spilling the water, which then meant I had to retrace my weary steps to fill the bucket again. And this time, I would be wet. However, we had our baths religiously every week because it was said that cleanliness was next to godliness.

During the winter, the wind swirled around the house and sang through the trees, but inside, it was warm and cosy with the turf burning away in the open fireplace. I always felt lucky and blessed to be born and live in such a beautiful place, the wonderful kingdom of Kerry, and for me, the jewel in the crown was Ballybunion. To this day, I think it is the most beautiful spot in Ireland, a little piece of heaven where I was wrapped in nature's beauty and in music.

My dad was a carpenter by trade and was thirty-one years of age when I was born. He had a gentle soul, a great heart and a lovely warm smile. He was my first hero. He was also a musician. We didn't have a television, which left us lots of time for conversation, stories and singalongs.

Dad's instrument was the accordion, and I loved it when he played it. It was always so nice to hear the sound of music and laughter ringing throughout the house. I had a strong bond with Dad from an early age, and we were really great friends. I always think of him when I hear songs like *The Gypsy Rover.*

We had a small number of animals on the farm: four cows, sometimes a few calves, a pig, ducks, hens, geese, a couple of dogs, a few cats and a lovely gentle donkey. I used to chat away with them all, but I had a special connection with the donkey, and he became my best friend. As a small child, I was very determined, and Dad often said I could be as stubborn as a mule. 'As God made them, he matched them,' he quipped, me and the donkey. When I got something into my head, I wouldn't let it go till I did what I wanted to do. No wonder Donkey and I were friends.

My older sister and I were quite different in temperament. She was bossy and spent a lot more time with Mum, doing things with her like cooking, baking, needlework, knitting and general housework. She was happier indoors, while I was more the outdoorsy type. It was probably just as well because it gave each of us our own space, and that seemed to suit both of us just fine.

I would go to sleep listening to the sounds of the farm animals and the wind rustling the leaves of the trees, and in the morning, I would be wide awake and wired as soon as I heard the cock crowing and the cows mooing. I was always up early, ready for a new day. Nan told me it was like I had an on-off switch—without the off part. I was impatient to be living life to the fullest and always had something to do or somewhere to go.

I was a sensitive child. For me, the seasons had different attractions, and I loved them all. In the spring, buds appeared and started to flower, the grass became more lush and green and animals birthed their babies. Sometimes I would wait for ages to see a new calf or lamb being born. It was an amazing experience, and I would watch with great interest as they struggled to take their first wobbly steps.

With each new day, they would get stronger and stronger till eventually you would see them running in the fields. In my young mind, I found it hard to reconcile how long it took my baby brothers and sisters to learn to walk compared to these animals who did it in a day!

Slowly, spring would turn to summer, and the countryside would be alive with life. By then, everything was in full bloom. It was warm, and I loved being able to wear lighter clothes.

Then came autumn, a time when we picked apples for eating and cooking and many types of berries for making jam and putting in pies. The leaves turned a golden brown and fluttered onto the paths and the roads and the meadows. The temperature was cooler—but not too cold—and if it was fine in the evenings, the sun would peep through the golden landscape, winking as if to say goodnight.

At that time, the swifts and swallows would circle around the house and perch on the wires preparing to head off on their holidays. They didn't like winter in Ireland and always went to places where they could enjoy the warm sun. However, I always knew one day they would come back. And they unfailingly did, year after year.

As autumn came to a close, you'd know it would not be long before you saw white smoke starting to meander out of chimneys as winter set in. Halloween came and went; then there was Christmas, a time of presents and tinsel and holly and ivy. In those cold months, the weather could vary from day to day. Some mornings could be frosty with the roads to school icy and slippery.

On other days, storms would rage, and cold winds howled through the hills and around our home. Dad said you would know what the weather would be like the next day by checking the light in the sky the previous evening. He would stand and gaze at the display of colours that shifted and changed as the sunset. He also would watch the moon in all its different stages and listen to the sounds of the sea in the distance. It was like Dad really understood the language of nature in all its different forms.

In every season, my sister and I helped Mum and Dad around the farm, and as the years went by, my younger siblings joined in too. My whole world was a playground with a new adventure every day. Now and again when we were playing in the puddles in the yard I would splash my sister and then run away, but mostly I behaved myself—or at least I tried to.

It was clear from the start that I loved animals and nature. The animals really responded to me and allowed me to get close to them and be their friend. At times in the summer, Donkey and myself would lie in the field resting my head on the donkey's neck as I looked up to the vast blue sky. I would just lie there daydreaming, with my many fleeting thoughts coining and going like the puffy white clouds going across the sky. My imagination painted pictures of unseen worlds beyond the mountains I might one day explore.

I wasn't at all squeamish and really didn't mind the sights or smells of the little farm. Even when I saw animals doing their business it didn't bother me. It was just nature, after all. I liked sitting on a large stone and looking at the big sow snuffling around or feeding her babies, and was also great to see the newborn calves drink milk from their mothers.

Sometimes we had to feed them out of a bucket and that was fun. The calves were deceptively strong, but I was a determined little thing and always managed to somehow hang onto the bucket. I also loved when the calves sometimes licked the palms of my hands with their coarse tongues.

The only creatures I didn't like too much were the geese, as they hissed at me and chased me around the farmyard if I bothered them. They were a little like my sister—easily annoyed.

Now and again, Mum would take me to a particular field we used to call the haggard at the back of the cottage. It had a small orchard in it, and in the summer, Mum and I used to sit on the grass and make daisy chains. Mum would sometimes pretend that I was a princess and would place a pretty daisy chain on my head like a crown. However, instead of playing along, I would go, 'Yuck!' and pull it off me. I was a feisty little thing, according to Mum, a bit of a tomboy.

Dad often took me for walks around the fields to see the animals and thought I was funny when I mimicked some of them. I loved to hear him laugh, and I miss him so much. His music and smiles filled so much of my life, and he brought joy and warmth into our house with the love that made it a home. The music, like the rest of us, has left the cottage now but the memories of Dad remain. It was a real privilege to be his daughter.

It is incredible to see how quickly time moves by. In recent years, I have gone back to visit the remnants of my old home and brought my granddaughter with me. I feel very lucky that I am able to retrace some of the walks that Dad used to take me on. However, my granddaughter is more of a lady than I was and is not as fond of the fields and the muck as I remember being back then.

My grand-uncle, Tady, was a tall man, thin as a lath, who would often carry me around up on his shoulders where I would be able to see all around me. My great-aunt, Hannah, who worked and lived in a hotel in Ballybunion, had a big horse which she kept on my dad's farm. Sometimes Tady would lift me up and put me on the horse's back. Then we would stroll around the field.

Eventually, he would say, 'That's it now,' but more often than not I would persuade him to do a few more rounds. Poor Tady! And even though the horse was big, there wasn't an ounce of fear in me. I just loved the experience and always wanted more.

I don't have many memories of my big sister in the early days because I was more focused on my own world. But in the years that followed, I became more aware of things and people around me, not least the arrival of younger siblings. Mum kept finding abandoned babies under cabbage leaves! First, there was a little boy called Timmy. He was so cute I could not imagine how someone could have left him under a cabbage leaf. My mum then went on to find a few more children in the same way, and I was so impressed that once I looked under the cabbages growing in our vegetable plots to see if I could find a baby of my own!

Of course, by the time the last ones came along I had discovered how babies were made.

Altogether there were seven of us in the family—three girls and four boys. The last boy was born when I was sixteen. Contraception in Ireland was not allowed by the Catholic Church in those days and parents were meant to welcome every child as a tremendous gift from God.

After all, God did say increase and multiply, and in truth, we were a happy lot and gave our parents laughs and merriment as we grew up.

One spring day, I decided my younger brother and I were going to go fishing. He was only too happy to come down to the little river with me and carried one of the two jars I was bringing along so that we would have something to put the fish in. I also carried a net to catch them with. It has to be said neither of us didn't know much about fishing at all, and we thought anything we found swimming in the water was a fish. My intention was to bring back something Mum could cook for dinner.

We tried dipping the net in the water for a while, but we had no luck with that, so then we used the jars. Slowly and gently, we sifted through the water and collected quite a few little wriggling things. We were delighted with ourselves and ran back home. But instead of being as thrilled as we were, Mum was less than impressed. 'They are not fish, they are tadpoles!' she shouted. 'Take them back where you found them!'

Disappointed by her lack of gratitude, the two of us sat morosely on the step for a while. In silence, we watched the little tadpoles swimming leisurely around in the jars. Then we made the heart-wrenching decision to go back to the river, and let them go, as Mum had instructed.

After our failed attempt as fishermen, we went on to temporarily capture other creatures in our jars from searching around in the fields. They included butterflies, ladybirds, spiders and several types of creepy-crawlies. The farm was full of them. I was always ready to experiment with things and tried to eat a worm once, but it wiggled on my tongue, and I ended up spitting it out.

At the time of the harvest, Dad would take me to where he created haystacks. They were like little mountains dotted throughout the fields. As he stacked them, he sometimes would put me up on top of one, and I would slide down it into his arms, screaming in delight. We had great fun laughing and playing together, and I would get Dad to do it again and again. My mum and sister would later come along with lunch, and we would all sit down by the haystacks in the fields. Mum would have tea in a jug with jam sandwiches and some of Nan's baked bread.

Spotted dick was my favourite, which is soda bread with sultanas or currants, and when it was eaten fresh out of the oven and spread with butter and jam, it just melted in your mouth. I would sometimes get more jam on my hands and face than in my mouth. Then my sister and I would run around the fields playing games like chasing and hide-and-go-seek. My parents always said these were the best days of our lives, and we should enjoy them. I really do have fond memories of those times.

During the summer, Mum would often take my sister and me to Ballybunion Beach. When we were younger she wheeled us down in the old-style pram which had small wheels at the back and bigger ones at the front. When we got older we would walk on either side of Mum. It was a three-mile journey, but it was worth it. We so looked forward to playing on the lovely sandy beach, a place I still love walking on today.

In the late afternoon, we would pack up and leave, and Mum would do her shopping on the way home. On the odd occasion, my sister and I would be given ice creams if Mum had enough money. The two of us would walk along happily licking our ice cream cones and getting ice cream on our cheeks and noses. They were a wonderful treat. Mum always liked to stop and talk to her friends and neighbours, as people were very friendly in the town back then and liked a good old chat.

There was never any rush to get anywhere quickly. As we walked home with the evening sun on us, we would pause to inspect and admire flowers that hung over the walls and also examined whatever else was worth investigating. We would skip and run and play on the pavement and the road. There weren't as many cars on the road back then, so we were quite safe. Sometimes my sister and I would be best of pals, sometimes not. But one thing was sure, we certainly had time to play, and every day brought a new adventure.

When we got home, Dad, Nan and Tady would be waiting for Mum to prepare dinner. Sometimes Nan and Tady would be in a bad mood, and they would shout at each other through the half-door. Their feistiness was a way of life for them. 'Just leave them at it,' Mum would say. It didn't take much of an excuse for Nan and Tady to go at one another in temper, which could end up with the two of them roaring and shouting at each other.

Nan's insults included threatening to knock Tady's block off. I didn't like fighting at all. That is, except with my older sister! So I do understand that sometimes brothers and sisters fight.

That's just families for you.

Anyhow, I was always determined nothing would destroy my time at the beach, and I could never wait to run and tell Dad all about our adventures and the wonderful things we had seen and done that day. When he finished work he usually relaxed with a cigarette in a comer of the main room, and when I came to him full of stories he always welcomed me with open arms and a big smile and listened attentively to what I had to say. As he and I engaged in conversation, Nan and Tady eventually calmed down from their exhortations. She'd go and sit in the other comer by the fire on her favourite stool, smoking a *duidin* (a clay pipe) and talking away to herself, and Tady would make himself scarce.

Because Nan could sometimes be grumpy I had a slightly strained relationship with her. Nonetheless, I still have some fond memories. When she sat on her stool she would always be poking at the turf in the fireplace in a quest for more heat. I often thought her black shawl would catch fire if she wasn't careful.

Above the fire was a crane for hanging the kettle on, and back in those days the kettle was usually on the boil, ready for anyone who wanted a cup of tea. She had a surprisingly young face and beautiful skin for someone I thought of as really old. Her grey hair was nearly always tied up in a bun, and she wore a lot of black clothes.

Nan was sixty-five years old when I was born, and I was the second baby coming into her home, which possibly irked her a bit. Even though Mum had me to mind, Nan wanted to be minded by my mother too, which meant less time for me. Poof Mum—she had enough things to do. She had to look after us kids and did her best to take care of Nan, Tady and all the animals as well. I now realise how hard she worked, and I am very grateful for all she did for us.

I was sometimes a little jealous that she and my sister seemed very close, but it was just a fact that she was more of a mammy's girl, while I was definitely a daddy's girl. Cooking, cleaning and housework were not my thing, as there were always so many more fun things to do and places to explore.

I was around seven years old when Nan died. In the area where we lived, the custom was to bum a recently deceased person's goods. It was my mother's mum, Gran, who was the decision-maker about this. I was distraught when I heard what they were going to do. I tried to save the shawl Nan often wore as well as a trunk that had belonged to her dad which had originally come from America. I remember it had small secret drawers in it.

Nan used to let me play with it now and again, and I used to hide my treasures in the little compartments. I couldn't understand why her things had to be destroyed and fought and screamed and got very angry about it. After all, the trunk had survived Nan's dad's death. But it was all to no avail. I was left broken-hearted, and it took me a long time to forgive Gran for burning Nan's things.

Funnily enough, today I love travel bags, cases and trunks. It probably comes as a subconscious compensation from that time.

I was aware of spirits as a child, and for a while after Nan died, I used to see her doing what she always did—sitting by the fire smoking her *duidin* and talking away to herself. My younger brother is sensitive too and one time stated he was at Nan's funeral. Mum told him that was impossible as he wasn't born then. However, my brother insisted he was there. He was actually able to give an accurate account of what happened at the funeral. Mum was pregnant with him at the time, so it certainly seemed like his little spirit was able to look around and see what was going on that day!

Shortly before Nan passed away, something strange happened. I woke up in the middle of the night and felt compelled to go to her room, which was unusual because nobody was allowed to disturb Nan when she was in her bedroom. As I stood there looking at Nan's sleeping form, the room suddenly filled with an amazing white light. Then Nan's spirit spoke to me and said that I would go on to have a special journey in my life. That was all—just those few words.

I also had the sensation of my hand being held by her. This was something I didn't understand at the time, but now I feel it was Nan's spirit preparing to go on a journey and needing to communicate with me before she left. We never had much time together as I was so often in the fields, and maybe she wanted to let me know, in spite of that, she still loved me and cared about me.

From early childhood, I remember being in hospital frequently with kidney infections. When I was very small the nurses put me in a cot-type bed that had iron bars on either side. I felt trapped, and I hated it. I tried to get out and shouted and screamed for Mum and Dad to rescue me, and was very upset when they didn't come.

I was too young then to know they couldn't stay with me all the time. I felt abandoned in this strange place with children I didn't know, and bossy people in odd clothes. I also wasn't used to the lack of freedom. As I grew up a bit, I got more used to being in hospital although I always felt lonely and homesick whenever I had to stay there.

One day, after another stint in hospital Mum came and brought me home. In the evening after dinner, I overheard her talking to Dad about what the doctor had told her that day. She had been horrified when the doctor asked if I had been interfered with. She was very upset and told the doctor that she didn't know whether I had been or not, and said she would do her best to get the bottom of the matter. I didn't understand what they were talking about at the time, but now I do. The frequent urinary tract infections I suffered as a child must have aroused suspicion in the doctor that I might have been sexually abused.

It turned out that the doctor had been right. Of course, I did not remember the earliest abuse, but I became aware of it as I grew up. Mum didn't get to the bottom of it and the abuse continued and was to have a detrimental effect on my bright personality over the ensuing years. The culprits (yes, there was more than one) were not my immediate family but were trusted individuals who lived nearby. Even today I can't fathom how anyone can hurt a child, but they do, and records show that lots of children are still at risk and need to be protected.

Back then we were not as conscious of abuse as we are today, and trust was often given to those who did not deserve it.

As I reflect on those days, I can see that Mum did her best and worked hard to keep the family going when things were tough. There is no doubt that the foundation of love and joy I got in those early days from my family was a true gift and helped carry and sustain me through many dark and bleak times throughout my life.

Chapter 2
A Stain on My Childhood

I can see now why my bright light faded. As I grew up, I began to feel isolated and unsafe and started to fade into the background, hiding, so I would not be hurt any more. I never found out who abused me as a very young child, and the truth of it all lies lost among the shadowy memories of the past. However, I do recall some of the incidents of abuse as an older child and as a young adult, and I have clear memories of who abused me at that time. I also realise that some of the abuse came with aggression and bullying, and other incidents were of a coercive nature.

These evil people watched my innocence disappear, not caring about the damage they were causing to a child. I hope someday they will answer for what they did to me, whether it is in this life or the next. I now realise that Mum and Dad had an awful lot of responsibilities on their shoulders at times, so I don't blame them for what happened to me. In those days, life was different, and it was nearly inconceivable to my parents that someone they trusted—a good neighbour or friend or part of an extended family—would even think of abusing a child. I just wasn't able to open up to my parents about what was happening to me no my shame, anger, pain and hurt built walls around me. I started to wash myself excessively to cleanse my body from its impurities and turned more and more inward.

I started to detach from life and disappeared into my own world. Because of this, I was actually more able to deepen my connection with the natural world around me. I was able to sense animals' thoughts and see spirits, angels and beings from the elemental world. To be honest, sometimes I wondered what was real and what was fantasy.

Did I just create imaginary friends to talk with or make up stories about fairies and earth spirits and animals to fill that void in me? Now, I know what I experienced was real. Fairies do exist, and I can tell you there are many different types of elemental beings in the world. I was also lucky to have been able to see angels from a very young age, and their brightness and joy were always a great source of comfort.

But when I told my Mum what I was seeing, she said I was imagining things.

'Many people have been placed in mental homes for hearing voices or seeing things that just aren't there,' she admonished me, 'so Kathleen, just stop now. Stop talking about it, or people will think you are odd.'

I knew I was not deranged or mad, and looking back now I can't help thinking of those poor people who used to be locked up in mental institutions for hearing and seeing things. I'm sure some of them were just super-aware of the spiritual world like me and didn't understand what was going on with them. I understand now that being able to see these special beings was God's and nature's way of minding me as a child, supporting me and showing me that I was not alone and never would be.

All the while that this was happening, the months and years passed. There is no pause button in life, no replay button for a child. One day's experiences merge into another and the collective memories go on to dictate who we are and how we portray ourselves to others. I only told Mum, Dad and a few people close to me I could see spiritual entities. I did get labelled as a bit odd, which made me sad.

I have to say I still experienced happy moments in the practical world. I tried my very best to have fun and not let the dark shadows control me or destroy my magic, and there were times, like all children, when I still managed to get into mischief and enjoyed childish adventures.

It was my friend Donkey who gave me my greatest comfort. We'd ride through the fields together, and sometimes we would go all the way down to the river and back up again. With him, I explored the natural world around the farm. I particularly loved keeping an eye on the birds that used to nest around the farm in the trees and bushes and in the eaves of the house. My heart would leap when I saw little baby birds peeping their heads out of their nests as their mums fed them with worms. And then there was this chatty little robin that frequently visited me in the farmyard and in the meadow.

Sometimes he would perch on Donkey's back and pull his hair. I'm not sure Donkey was pleased with the robin, but it was very funny to see a little bird riding on a donkey. I know now that the robin was probably using Donkey's hair to line his—or her—nest. On my many journeys with my friend, we often saved little animals which were being hunted. It could be a mouse that was being chased by a cat, or a fox chasing a rabbit. I was having none of it. It was Donkey and I to the rescue.

He was so funny, and a lot cleverer than you'd think. He seemed to know everything that was going on at the farm on any given day. When he heard the rest of the family coming, Donkey would run away from them, but when I was around, he would come to me. He would not let anyone on his back except me. They all tried to get on him, but he would throw them off and then would hee-haw with glee at them.

I always found myself laughing along with him. There would be some angry red faces from my siblings when this happened, and I suppose I should not have laughed, but I just couldn't help myself. I have to admit it was good to have this special friendship with an animal who obviously thought I was special too.

My relationship with my older sister, Nan's pet, was often difficult. We were near in age and there was a bit of sibling rivalry between us. We were in essence fighting for our space in the family, but it has to be said she was very bossy indeed. I do understand it was all part of growing up, and I still love her.

Then school happened. I used to smugly smile as I watched my sister leave first thing in the morning with her satchel and lunch, knowing I was free to roam, and she wasn't. But one morning that changed. That day, Mum, my sister and I stood outside a cold stone building, and I now carried a satchel and packed lunch, just like my sister.

The school was in Lisselton, about three miles away from our house. So this was the place my sister had done so much moaning about. I saw the kids from the area, some accompanied by their mothers, traipsing through the school doors. I did not like the idea of going in there at all and began to backtrack. Mum grabbed me.

‘Come on now, Kathleen,’ she said. ‘Let’s go and meet the nice lady teacher.’

She pulled me forward, and it wasn’t long before I was sitting in a classroom with a bunch of other children. Our seats were wooden benches, and in front of us were long desks where we put our copybooks. The setup was typical of a country school at the time. Our school had three classes in one room and the teacher sat at the top of the classroom behind a desk. A blackboard was on the wall beside her.

On that first day, I spent more time looking out the window than listening to the teacher, trying to think of ways of escaping. It didn’t take me long to realise that there weren’t any. This was my life—school—for what looked like forever. I sat there, forlorn, miserable and trapped.

Eventually, in time I grew used to the routine. Thankfully, a lot of the kids were nice, and I made some good friends during my incarceration. However, I thought reading and writing were boring and found it hard to sit still. I asked to go to the toilet a lot just to leave the classroom. It was always a bit of an adventure going outside to the small stone outhouse at the end of the school garden—anything to lift the boredom.

The bowl of the toilet was far wider than I was and there was no wooden or plastic seat to sit on. Overhead there was a big cistern for the water and a chain I had to pull to flush. It was quite a tricky task to sit balanced on the side of the bowl while doing my business, and then afterwards to jump up and down several times before I could catch the chain and give it a good tug. The toilet was dirty and smelly from years of use by all the children in the school. It was the opposite of home, where I used the far more hygienic and pleasant grassy areas behind the bushes.

Whenever I answered the call of nature this way I used to enjoy looking at all the beauty around me—the green lush flora and the cows, the birds and the butterflies. I admit it wasn't great in wet or windy weather, and in those cases, I just did my business as quickly as possible and ran back into the house. I didn't hang about when the wind was coming down off the hills.

When the weather was cold, open fires would be lit in the classrooms. On those days, the children brought turf in with them so the fires could be kept going. We also left our bottles of tea near the fire, so they would stay warm. We'd have our lunch at school, usually jam sandwiches and tea.

Sometimes we wrote our name, made a mark or drew a picture on the bottle to show it was ours. Ireland was poor back then, especially in the country, and unfortunately, it wasn't unusual for your bottle of tea to disappear because some child who was even less well off than you would have swiped it.

I understood that education had to be taught and that it was good to learn, but I felt that was for other people, not me. I wanted freedom and was not best pleased to be stuck in school. It was not where I wanted to be. I was used to being a free spirit, constantly on the move and looking for adventure, not looking for a rubber to erase a spelling mistake in my textbook. I felt like a prisoner with little or no chance of parole. As it was, I rarely paid attention.

Sometimes I'd try to wander in the classroom, but of course, I'd always get told to sit down. Fed up, I'd then lose myself in daydreams and imagine myself walking through the haggard, playing with Donkey, jumping in puddles or talking to the fairies. I'd try to be anywhere else but where I was. At the end of the school day, as soon as the bell went, I'd run home to my friend, Donkey, and we'd be off on our next adventure.

I liked my first two teachers and tried to learn from them. They were lovely women with real gentle and caring energy, and their names were Crissy and Carmel. I'll remember them fondly always, and because of the way they were, I did learn some things in school. I suppose if you sit there long enough, you're bound to learn something!

The other teachers were more stern, and one or two were bullies. I remember being in the school on one particular day and seeing a male teacher beating the heck out of a young boy. It is hard to believe now that abuse like this actually happened, but punishment was allowed in those days, and children didn't have anyone they could report to if they felt were unfairly treated.

If you mentioned to your mum or dad that a teacher in school hit you, they'd most likely say, 'Well, that saved me the bother. You must have done something to deserve it.' But no child deserved what I saw that day, as the teacher hit the child so hard that he actually drew blood. The memory of that event is still etched in my mind today.

One morning, my friend Maura, who was always up for a bit of devilment, and I decided we would play truant. Just before we reached school we ran off and hid. When we knew the coast was clear and all the kids were in school we wandered around exploring and munching berries we picked from the hedgerow. All in all, we thoroughly enjoyed our stolen freedom. Little did we know we were spotted by one of the teachers.

We were unaware of this and when we went to school the next day, we giggled with glee in thinking we had got away with our little escapade. Then a couple of days later our class teacher made us stand up in front of the whole class and said, 'Well, ladies, did you enjoy your day off?'

We had been caught. Our faces went bright red as everyone looked at us. We were not only mortified but were afraid we might be caned or sent to the headmaster, a real grump. God knows what punishments he would give us! Luckily, after a few stern words about truancy and the effects of not going to school in the future, the teacher let us sit down and that was it. We still worried for a few days after that, but nothing happened.

As our teacher seemed to have eyes in the back of her head, we thought better of mitching again. Moreover, we did not want to test fate as we thought we might not escape so lightly next time. The sounds of the cane, or sally rod, swinging in the breeze could be quite frightening in the hands of any strict teacher.

One evening, we were all midway through our dinner when Dad came in. Sometimes he was late to the table because of some job or other he was doing, so that was nothing unusual. But then I noticed his solemn demeanour as he sat down beside me. With tears in his eyes, he looked at me and said, 'I'm so sorry, Kathleen, your donkey is dead.'

Dad had a soft heart and was sad when any of the animals died, but he knew that I loved Donkey and was concerned about how I would take this tragic news. But to his surprise, I just shrugged my shoulders and went back to my dinner. I know now I was in shock, but it showed how much I had shrunk into my isolated world even then. I had become so independent and self-reliant I did not admit, even to myself, that I needed anyone or anything as it would be a sign of weakness or vulnerability.

Today, I am lucky enough to own a beautiful dog named Alex. If anything happened to him, I would be in absolute bits, but at least I know that now I am able to express my feelings freely. I have come a long way. Back then I had closed my heart and held my emotions inside. I did actually grieve Donkey in my own way.

I didn't eat for a week and walked around the farm in a lonely cloud, unaccountably angry with the animal for leaving me and terribly sad we would have no more fun times together. For some time afterwards, I used to think I heard him braying in the early mornings, singing his song to get me to wake up and come out to play.

Dad knew the way I reacted to his news about Donkey's death was not normal behaviour because he knew I loved the animal so much and as a result was worried about me. One day he took me for a walk through the fields and brought me to where Donkey lay buried. On the way, we collected some flowers for his grave. Amazingly, the little robin who had often joined Donkey and me on our travels was sitting near where Donkey was buried.

It was like he was sad and lonely too for his lost friend. The flowers we collected were daisies and sweet rocket, a flower that comes in shades of white, pink, purple and blue. I placed them on Donkey's grave, and we said a short farewell prayer. It was the end of an era for me.

I think I grieved the loss of my friend more and more through the years, as in daydreams my mind would wander back to my many adventures with this gentle creature. I know death is part of life and that children must eventually understand that, but it is hard nonetheless. It was especially difficult for me because I wasn't able to openly express my sorrow. How could they understand?

I cannot get over how quickly I withdrew from the family and into my own world, and how easily I learned not to trust or attach to anyone or anything. I never seemed to belong. As I grew up, I lived with abuse and abandonment as if it was all part of normal life and learned that it was up to me to look after myself and protect myself. No one else was going to do it for me. Throughout my childhood and my days at school, I tended to be fearful and shied away from people rather than joining in and having fun. I do remember funny and sunny moments, but they are isolated incidents.

Sometimes these glimpses into the past are hard because they come back with memories that forced me to detach in the first place. But then some happy memories, lost amongst the shadows and pain, have also begun to re-emerge. When this happens I find myself giggling and crying in equal measure. I allow them to sit and take time with them, and in this way, I help my heart to heal. Using my experience of life, the adult me can help the child rue make different choices and gain a greater understanding of what happened. I can't emphasise enough that all children are vulnerable and need to be protected from the dangers that lurk in damaged adults.

I know these events were not my fault and gradually, as I started to discover my inner child by clearing my trauma and conditioning over time, I am no longer ashamed of myself or of who I am. Now I am proud of the little girl I was then and of the courage she had to survive and not let the abusers win.

As I shine a light on the darkness of the past, I see myself bum brighter and brighter, and I know it is this light that is leading me back to the precious child I was created to be. It would be nice if I could have total recall of my memories, but that is just not the way it works. There seems to be only so much awareness that the angels think I am able to handle at any given time, so I hope you will bear with me as my sketchy history is slowly pieced together. My memories unfold bit by bit so that I can heal in manageable stages. As I find renewed purpose, belief and freedom in my life, I feel grateful for the learning these qualities give me, and I am happy with the gift of tomorrow.

One of the things I would love to do someday, when the time is right, is adopt or buy a little donkey. It would be a wonderful present to myself, and verification that I am starting anew. As the past loses its grip on my future, both my inner child and my present adult look forward to enjoying life once again with clarity, strength, freedom, and the knowledge that I am safe.

Chapter 3
Friendship with the Fairies

In school, life settled down and was tediously predictable. I couldn't avoid it, so had to put up with it. I understood that reading, writing and maths were useful to learn, but how much reading, writing and counting does one need in life? After all the hard work in class, I always looked forward to break times when I was able to let off steam and play games like chasing, hopscotch, tag and skipping with the other kids.

At lunchtime, I would go to my gran's house, which was nearby. She was my mother's mother. I loved her bubble and squeak (cabbage, potatoes and onions laden with butter), and sometimes Gran would give me my favourite treat which was home-made apple pie. Then too soon I had to run back to school. The bell rang, and we were all lined up again and went back to class. Finally, after watching the clock beat out its long seconds for what seemed forever, the school day ended, and we would all escape to freedom from the shackles of our desks.

The first thing that had to be done when sis and I got home were the chores, which included sweeping, fetching water from the well, feeding the fowl, and helping mum hang out clothes on the line or take in clothes that were dry. Then there were days when we were sent to get groceries in the local shop, which was three miles away. Carrying them back home was tough because they got heavier and heavier with each passing minute. We would be pretty tired by the time we got home but no one ever listened to any of our complaining or whining. It was just a chore that had to be done.

After that, we had to do our homework (as if we didn't do enough work in class!), and if I had any time to spare after that, I would spend it out in the fields. Then it was time for our evening meal, and afterwards, we all might have a chat. Then before you knew it, it was time for bed.

This pattern continued week after boring week. From Monday I was looking forward to the weekend, and on Sunday evenings came the dread of Mondays again and facing another long week ahead, except on holidays or if I was sick. At times, I felt very controlled and did not like it one bit. Some freedom came at the weekends, but you could never have a lie-in in our house. There was always something to do.

Anyway, I was never one to stay in bed, and I didn't really mind helping out. At least I wasn't at school. For that reason, it was always a little easier and sweeter getting up on Saturday and Sunday mornings.

During the winter, the weather was often too bad to play outdoors at school break times, and we'd get twitchy and irritated with each other by the time we were back home in the afternoon. We were just suffering from cabin fever and had nowhere to vent or release our excess energy.

'It'll be spring soon,' Nan told us. 'The weather will get better and the days will be longer, and you'll be running through the fields before you know it.'

But patience was not my strong point. I never understood why the sun went to bed earlier in the winter than it did in the summer. I used to think that if I was big and bright, I'd like to stay up as long as I could. Maybe it was feeling fed up like me, with the cloudy and wintry days. But of course, thank God, winter would come to an end, and we did eventually see the lengthening days, the easing of the cold weather and new life spreading over the land.

The changing seasons created different vistas in nature and like a picture postcard Cnoc an Óir wore different looks according to the seasons and the moods and vagaries of the weather. I marvelled at nature and the incredible beauty of it all as the landscape daily changed in front of our eyes.

'There is a time for all things,' my father used to say. He was a wise man and someone I learned an awful lot from. 'There is a time to rest and play, a time to plant and sow, a time to grow, a time to harvest and bring the harvest home, and a time to let the land rest, all in God's good time.'

This was really another way of saying all was in divine timing and divine order. It's only now as I come to understand my life's journey that I see God is in charge, and I need to accept and embrace changes as they come along.

As spring arrived, I loved nothing more than going to the small orchard where the apple trees, blackberry bushes and gooseberry bushes started to bring forth blossoms. It was just a lovely time of year. Then in autumn, Mum and I would pick the ripened fruits and berries, and I got many a scrape on my legs or stung by nettles as I reached into briars for the juiciest blackberries. As I filled my bucket, I was always very fair—one for me, one for the bucket.

Mum would say: 'Be careful, Kathleen, your eyes are bigger than your belly. You'll have no room left for dinner.' But I always did. I didn't mind the nettles too much as I knew from when I was very young that if I was stung I would always use the milk from a dock leaf stem (always found near nettles) and that would take the sting out of the nettle attacks. I would be left with a few white bumps on my legs and arms, and they disappeared within an hour or two. I was a hardy wee thing back then and still am today.

Some of our apples were for eating straight off the tree, and some were for cooking. Nan used to make delicious apple tarts when the cookers were in season. I tried eating a bit of a cooking apple once while Nan filled a pastry base with apple slices, but it was very bitter, and my face scrunched up with the taste.

'Why didn't you stop me?' I complained.

Nan just laughed. 'That's how you learn,' she said. 'Your face was a picture.'

My face went bright red with anger but then I got distracted as I watched Nan working expertly on the pie. She shook some sugar over the apples and carefully placed a circle of rolled-out pastry over the pie. After gently pushing down on the edges to seal it, she cut away the excess pastry with a knife and then crimped down the sides of the pie. Then she popped it in the oven and cleaned up everything, washing the bowl and utensils and putting away all the ingredients. While it was baking, the kitchen was filled with a beautiful aroma, and any irritation that remained in me vanished when the pie came out of the oven, and I was given a slice. It was scrumptious.

I used to love baking pretend cakes out in the field. Mud cake pies with worms were my favourite, and sometimes Dad would join me for tea. I'd tell him, 'You see I'm baking just like Nan.' Dad would smile graciously, hold the mud pie up to his mouth and go, 'Num num num.' I knew he was only pretending to eat, but it was good fun, and I really appreciated when he gave me time like this. It made me feel really valued by him.

Up until a certain age, I thought everyone saw beings from the elemental kingdom. I was able to see all sorts of little people dressed in many different ways. Some had wings, others didn't. I knew they were real, but it felt odd when I realised that no one else could see them but me. I also used to hear the banshee howling when a neighbour or friend was going to die.

I was never comfortable when I heard her mournful cry and Mum tried to reassure me, saying I was just probably hearing the wind whistling through the trees. But I knew it wasn't the wind, and that it was a communication to me that grief was coming to our land. The next day, as sure as eggs are eggs, someone in our small community would pass away. It was not something I could prevent or warn other people about. It was just a message.

Why I alone heard it, I don't know. It was just the way it was. I know now I was allowed to hear this news from Spirit to teach me to be receptive and trust and to get me used to communications from them.

Along the way, I found out that Gran's brother, my great-uncle Willie, also had special abilities. Even though we did not see him often I really liked him and felt connected to him. I now know that part of it was because we were both very sensitive and intuitive. As well as that, Uncle Willie was a really nice man.

One day, Mum decided to take me on a visit to Uncle Willie's home. Gran and my uncle lived about four miles away in Ballydonaghue, near the village of Lisselton. Sometimes Mum would roll her eyes when talking about him. I think she was a little frightened of him and his gifts.

'That uncle of mine can be a bit strange,' she would say. 'Don't mind him and his wild stories. I know you are special, Kathleen, but don't become weird like he is.'

Willie was of average height, quite slight and balding but had lovely clear shiny skin. He also had a kind demeanour and a ready smile. His hugs were warm and welcoming, and I knew I could trust him. He loved to see us when we came to visit. Willie always had time for me, and I really appreciated that.

He was a great man, and I didn't find him strange at all. He had worked in England like a lot of Irish men did at that time, particularly as there was little or no work available locally, but when his mother needed minding, he took the first boat back home. He set his own life aside when his mum needed him. That was just the sort of man he was. He had a real caring and loving nature.

The house was always immaculate and very peaceful. Unlike Tady and Nan, Willie and his mum never seemed to fight or niggle with each other. I got the impression they were happy and content in each other's company, and I always looked forward to seeing them.

It was Uncle Willie who told me he knew I was able to see elementals and that I had a special gift which wasn't given to everyone. When I told him how surprised I was that no one else I knew could see them he just said, 'Through the years, Kathleen, I've come to realise that only some people have this gift. Some, like us, are open to having these friendly little visitors come to them. So don't worry about it. Just enjoy seeing them and having this special gift.

'And you don't need to fear them. Learn to become their friends and play with them, and they will learn to trust you and play with you too. In time, you will come to learn their true value to you and the world. It will strengthen your gifts,' he added, 'and it will definitely have something to do with your life purpose, which no doubt will be spiritual in nature.'

Not only could Uncle Willie see and sense the spirit world, but he was also a gifted diviner and could quite easily find fresh water wells for people on their land. Using nothing but his intuition, he would stand in a certain spot in a field and tell the landowner that water would be found there, so many feet underground. When the landowner would dig, he invariably would find water as fresh and pure as the land it came from.

One day, Uncle Willie took me for a walk around his land. He brought me over to some trees and told me to feel the life in them by putting my hand on a tree trunk. At first, I giggled, but when I saw that my uncle was absolutely serious I placed my hand on the tree. To my astonishment, a moment later I felt a tingle and a strange type of movement up and down the knot of the tree. When I told him this he was delighted.

'Now you see, Kathleen,' he said. 'The trees are alive, everything is. Being as intuitive as you are. I just knew you would be able to feel this. I have a special gift for you that I'll hide away in a place that no one will find before its time. And when the time is right you will come to understand more. Till then it will be our little secret.'

I knew not to enquire further, and we turned and walked back to the house. To be honest, I was just happy enough to have acknowledgement of my sensitive nature by this simple yet wise and humble man. It was like my abilities were part of an ancient history within my family, inherited from the past.

I never did get whatever Uncle Willie had hidden for me. Maybe the gift actually lay in the recognition and validation of me, and if so, I am forever grateful for that.

It was a good long walk back to Ballybunion after our visit that day, but I didn't mind. I had my little friends walking beside me along the hedgerows. Some tiny goblins would pull weird faces at me, and I would pull faces back at them. The fairies would also fly around me, but I didn't want to engage with them too much because Mum would think I was mad!

Some years later, Uncle Willie had to go to a nursing home as he couldn't look after himself any more. At this stage, he was living alone as his mother had died some years before. His sister, my grandmother, also went to the same nursing home as she had developed dementia. One evening I went to visit them both. Uncle Willie was not in the living room area where he would normally sit, and the carer told me he was not well and was in his room.

When I went in I saw my mother, my aunt and uncle around his bed. His breathing was laboured and shallow and the poor man was desperately unsettled. It nearly broke my heart to see him like that. Mum saw me and moved aside, so I could be near him. His eyes were closed and, gently taking his hands, I told him I loved him and found myself saying it was time to release the silver strings that were binding him to Earth.

This was purely intuitive, but now I understand the importance of giving loved ones permission to go. Then I kissed him on his head, and a few moments later he gently slipped away. It was as if he had been waiting for me to say goodbye.

After a short while, I said to the others I was going to visit Gran, who resided in a different part of the nursing home. It was a very dark night and the old lady was sitting looking out the window.

'I can see Willie in the clouds,' she said sadly to me. 'He has gone home, Kathleen.' All I said was, 'Yes, Gran, I know.'

Mum had asked me not to say anything about Uncle Willie's death as she thought it might upset Gran, but Gran knew already. From her few words, I knew that my uncle was free and at peace in heaven.

With Uncle Willie gone, my connection to Ballydonaghue ended. But that lovely man will always remain in my heart. He taught me that it was OK to be me, to be able to see and feel things that others can't and to bridge the dimensions of different worlds.

'Kathleen, you are sensitive,' that's all I remember him saying to me. 'It's just normality for us. Don't let anyone make you think you are strange or mad. You're not.'

Allowing me my own identity was so important because I know now that all children need acceptance and affirmation. What Uncle Willie did for me was plant the seed of my faith in my gift for use today. I really don't think there is any more precious gift you can give to an invisible child than recognition, and his acceptance was the best gift ever. Thank you, Uncle Willie, for being part of my life.

I was becoming more “weird” around this time, according to my family. My inability to talk about the abuse caused me to become increasingly withdrawn and lost. School was actually a welcome break at times from the unwanted attention I received from some people around my area. But as time went by I realised that to help myself I had to stand up for myself more.

I discovered that when I projected an energy of anger to those who intimidated me, it helped me to protect myself. I noticed that when I became physically aggressive, people would often retreat and move away. I would then run to a safe place or go to someone I could trust.

Unfortunately, the latter were few and far between. Often they unknowingly let me down and that would compound my feelings of isolation and abandonment.

So I lived in two very separate but parallel universes. A small blessing was that when I was in nature I was able to be my innocent and carefree self. I doted on my animal friends, marvelling at their beauty. I loved seeing butterflies and was always on the lookout for different kinds, and on a few occasions, I saw some blue butterflies which weren’t common in our area. I also used to enjoy letting little ladybirds scurry over my hands after I borrowed them from grasses and bushes.

I watched in fascination as spiders created their webs, and was always on the lookout for hedgehogs in the undergrowth. They were funny little creatures who could curl up into a spiky little ball if they felt under threat. (I used to think it would be nice if I could do the same at times.) Whenever I explored this wonderful world on my own, I never felt alone, and I knew that as I was celebrating nature, nature was celebrating me.

As well as being sensitive to the land, Dad was very much in touch with Spirit. He once told me of a spirit that regularly visited him on the land, but tended to avoid this type of conversation in front of Mum. He was very interested in the cycles of the moon and how they affected nature and people. He also used to say the stars had lots of wisdom.

I used to sit there, spellbound, listening to every word from my hero, my dad. 'Did you know, Kathleen, the North Star has guided sailors home for centuries?' he said to me one time. He told me on another occasion that if I heard the sea roaring from our back door a life was going to be taken at sea. I do remember this happening a couple of times. The voice of my dad has echoes of the knowledgeable old Irish farmer, and as I write this, I am cognisant of this being the first of February, St Bridget's Day.

On this day, Dad would bless the land and the house. It was just something he did, part of his tradition. It is clear now that my intuitive gifts came from both my mum and dad. Mum didn't really talk about her gifts because she was a bit afraid of them, but they were in her family nonetheless.

I used to sometimes be a bit puzzled as a child: how come people accepted my dad's and uncle's special gifts, while I was the one who was considered odd? As the saying goes, 'There's nothing so strange as folk.'

In more recent times, people have asked me how parents don't get curious and ask questions when they see a sharp change in their child's personality. Personally, I think the adults may be detached on a few levels. Maybe they put the child's discontent or unhappiness down to a phase or a stage the child is going through. Personally, I think that was the conclusion my parents came to.

'It is hard to deal with her when she is in one of her moods,' I'd hear them say.

They would sometimes quote that nursery rhyme line: 'When she is good, she is very very good and when she is bad, she is horrid.' I'd also sometimes be seen as being "away with the fairies". In truth, I didn't need to go anywhere with the fairies as they were already there with me. It was a pity Mum and Dad did not see the hurt little child that I was. They seemed to come to the conclusion that their daughter had a great heart but a ferocious temper. They did not hear or see my cries for help.

And the sad thing was, no matter how much I looked for their attention and care, I could not tell them what was happening. I just did not have the language. How little they really knew me.

At the end of the day, maybe some parents don't question a child's changed behaviour too much lest in looking under rocks they might find things they do not want to see, and so instead they live in a tragic state of denial.

Chapter 4
Changing Worlds

Someone once said that the only guarantee in life is change. Never were truer words spoken. At the age of five, Tady suddenly disappeared from my life. No one told me what had happened to him. He just vanished out of the house and out of my world, never to be seen again.

I remember looking around the farm for him to no avail. It was to be a few years before I found out that he had died, passed into spirit. I must have been left at home when the funeral took place as my parents probably thought I was too young to understand what happened.

Children's feelings were rarely considered in situations like this back then but let me tell you, children understand and know a lot more than you'd think, and they can grieve the loss of a loved one more than you know. For me, not knowing what happened to a person who had been a real part of my life for five years was harder to accept than if I had been told he was going back to Holy God. Today, we know how important it is to support children during times of loss and grief when someone they loved has passed, but back then, there just wasn't any understanding of the pain of a child.

As time went by, I received information about Tady's untimely disappearance. He had gone to hospital suffering from TB and cancer, and that kind, caring and sensitive man actually paid for his own care, so he could make my mother's life a bit easier. She would not have to care for him. He knew it was an extra responsibility she could do without.

I do recall Tady's disappearance, but I blocked out a lot of my other childhood recollections. It is only in recent times that some of these memories are coming back to me. This shows how much I detached from what was going on around me as a child. It was the only way I could cope with the bad memories in my life. It took a huge effort to put some of these memories and feelings back together again, to recognise and honour them.

Through those years, I was not a happy bunny. My need to find my own space was important as it had become my way of avoiding pain and hurt and dealing with any perceived danger or threats around me.

There was a small bridge over the river near our house, and I discovered that the space under the bridge was a perfect hideaway. This was a place where I could be at peace and not be disturbed. I would take my wellies, put on an old coat, grab my favourite tea set and spend time with my elemental friends who lived in this magical place. I was just five when I first went there, and because it was well sheltered from the elements I could go there hail, rain, or shine.

To get there, I had to walk over rocks. They were almost like stepping stones strategically placed by Mother Nature, so I wouldn't get my feet wet. When I arrived at my designated spot, ironically enough, I would sometimes jump in the water and splash all around me.

Mum used to say the rats might bite me, but they never came too close, and I was never afraid of them anyway. I was used to seeing them around the farm, and they always tended to keep their distance and run away when they saw me coming. When I was down by the river I occasionally heard a rustle from the foliage and now and again I caught a glimpse of a rat looking at me and then off it would scurry.

Anyway, I had my little friends with the power of their magic to protect me, so I would just get on with my tea party and chat away with them. I used to sit on a big slab of flat stone and there I would set up my kitchen and imagine I was a queen entertaining friends in my own secret kingdom. Of course, we were all polite to each other. Wasn't that the way tea parties should be?

I always felt safe while I played underneath the bridge. It was like Mother Nature stood guard over me. Here was a place where this little human and nature lived harmoniously, a place where I had peace and stillness and was sheltered and happy out. As I sat there, I would hear the occasional clip-clop and clatter overhead of the caravans drawn by cob horses and the chatter of holidaymakers making their way around the beautiful scenery of Ballybunion during summer.

As well as having tea parties with the little beings of nature sometimes I would just sit and talk to them. As in all families, there were lots of different characters. Some were a bit rambunctious and could pull funny faces, others were shy and reserved, and others were joyful and mischievous. All were welcome, with no exclusions. I also liked it when the angels came to visit.

First I would hear a flutter of wings and then I would see a gentle caring face. One particular one came more than the others, and I think she might have been my guardian angel. I also loved playing with the various different wildflowers and plants along the riverbank. They included daisies, buttercups, dandelions, grasses, ferns, reeds and rushes. As far as I was concerned, they were there to beautify my surroundings, a gift from the fairies who were the custodians of the natural world.

This was not a place for other people—it was only for me. I never tolerated invaders in my special place. My sister and brothers knew that and never intruded. I think they were afraid of being on the receiving side of my anger if they did! When I was under the bridge I often lost all sense of time. Looking back, I am aware of how different it was there.

When I went under the bridge the water stopped flowing and only when I stepped back on the bank did the water start flowing again. It was like switching a tap on and off, so to speak. What a wonderful gift it was to experience the magic of the fairy people in their realm. It was a privilege I will never forget.

Mum usually knew where I was if she wanted me. When I heard her shouting out my name I would usually ignore her. She always seemed to be looking for me to do this or that or go here or there. To this day, I hate anyone keeping tabs on me and trying to control me, trying to tell me what to do. I tend to do what I want to do anyway. "Live and let live" is my motto.

Mum would probably say I was too independent. I felt sorry for Dad because Mum sometimes gave him a real ear-bashing about the way I was. I now know that, like my Uncle Willie, Dad was intuitive and aware of the fairy folk and spirits. It was such a relief to know they believed I felt and saw these things.

I knew my dad understood me and wasn't at all worried about me. We were kindred spirits, cut from the same cloth, but my mother, well, she could be a different story altogether. She was earthed, efficient and focused. She tried to keep me grounded, but that was never going to work.

It's got to be said I didn't mean to upset Mum when I was awkward with her. She was a good mother and great to be around most of the time, but when I heard my elemental friends calling me or felt their need to be with me, I had to go to them. It was just something I had to do. I am a mum myself now and know that my mother was trying to do her best and was concerned I would grow up odd or different and might be laughed at.

'This world is not an easy place to live for those who are different or don't fit in,' she would say. It turned out that she had no need to worry at all, as communicating with spirits turned out to be my life's work. Looking back, I suppose life might have been different if I hadn't been given the gift of intuitive sight and if I hadn't been abused and had never felt abandoned. But that was not the way my journey was meant to be.

When I realised people didn't sense and see the elemental world like I did, I didn't really mind. To be honest, I valued my gift all the more and liked the fact that I could see things others couldn't, especially my sister. But it became clear that people in general didn't believe in this other world, and I found it was wiser to keep quiet about it. I have also discovered that for some people, seeing is believing, and even if they do glimpse something strange or different, they still look for rational explanations for it. What a pity we cannot accept people as they are. The world would be a happier place for us all if we did.

It used to amaze Mum how long I could spend under the bridge and how I would come up from the river dry and relatively clean. I would not even be as mucky as I would be when I was just hanging around the farm. I had friends in school, and I was happy to play with them, but when I came home, there was nothing I liked more than playing games with the fairies. To this day, I have never experienced the same peace and stillness I enjoyed when I was in the loving care of Mother Nature and my magical friends.

It was three years after Tady passed away that Nan died. By this time, I had a better understanding of death and dying. She died just when we were all moving house. Our new abode was built in what had been the haggard, where we had our little orchard. Nan hadn't wanted to move from her home and, like me, did not want our orchard destroyed.

It was a place she loved her whole life and which held so many precious memories for her. I personally think Nan decided there was no way she was moving to the new house; she was just not interested in a new world without her little cottage and surrounding orchard.

Before she died, she said, 'We may be getting new-fangled things like indoor toilets, baths and running water, but we are losing our lovely home as well as the orchard.' I heartily echoed her sentiments.

One morning, during those last days in the cottage, a yellow machine pulled up. I remember it was very big and noisy. It was a bit like a tractor, but this machine had a box for the driver and a scoop in the front. With great sadness, I watched as it scraped the earth and started destroying the orchard.

My fairy friends told me they were very unhappy about this. They said their relatives who lived in that beautiful haggard would have to leave home and find somewhere new to live. I felt so forlorn on their behalf. There is nothing worse than seeing your friends upset and not being able to do anything about it.

'It's very clear that some people don't respect our world,' the little beings said ruefully, and I could feel their pain and their sense of loss. I could only imagine what other fairies felt like in developing towns and cities, where they were made homeless probably every day.

With the machines came workmen with shovels and picks, and fags hanging from their lips. Others came with chainsaws, and they started to attack the trees in the haggard. Every time a tree fell I winced for my friends. I could almost hear the trees cry as they were cut down and cleared away till all the orchards and all the fruit bushes were gone. There would be no more eating or cooking our home-grown apples.

Gone was the place I used to play in. Gone was the place where Mum and I used to sit and make daisy chains. I felt my whole world was ripped apart. There were holes in the ground everywhere. I was so angry with the workmen and not happy with Mum and Dad because they let them do this.

After the digger came to dig the foundations for the new house, I knew there was no going back, but what price progress? We were going to have electricity for the first time and plumbing was going to be installed so that we would no longer have to take water from the well. Soon the floors of the new house went in along with the walls, windows and doors and finally the day came when everything was done, and we had a new house. Oh, there was great excitement that day, with most of my family totally unaware of the pain of the land or of the fairies.

I didn't feel much joy either as it was a whole new world with no Nan, no Tady, no orchard. It was just me and the rest of the family and a new house. Whoop de doo. Now we were a posh family with indoor running water, an inside loo and a bathroom. But no gooseberries, blackberries and apple pies made by Nan.

The first time I went inside the house, I thought it was filthy. It was absolutely covered with dust everywhere but slowly over time the place took shape, and it became fresh, clean and dust-free. For me, though, it wasn't home. It was just a house without history. The little cottage was my home with the half doors and the big warm fire in the hearth and Nan and Tady and all of us squished in together, and the kettle always on the boil.

I found it hard to settle and cried myself to sleep many nights after the new house was finished. But, gradually, we all got used to living there. We grew accustomed to going to the loo inside as well as having hot and cold running water and being able to take baths and showers whenever we wanted. Soon we had all the mod cons such as a radio, TV and even a fridge! But I often spent long moments daydreaming and remembering the good times at the cottage and ruefully wondering what was going to come next.

What helped and comforted me were my friends under the bridge. I told them all of my worries and fears, and they listened and were sympathetic. They could feel my pain and knew at least that one human cared about the devastation that was going on around them. They also talked to me about other times when they had to readjust when humans destroyed their land and built on it, and how it made them so sad. They were fearful that the days of humans living in empathy with them, and their land was over. They said that if people were not careful they might lose a lot more than they gained in the future and communications between the worlds might be lost forever.

I didn't like school that much, I am sure you get that by now! But I did learn to read and write, and I know the teachers did their best to transform me into a good little woman who conformed and fitted into certain norms. But I was not made like that. I was an independent girl, now entering my teenage years. The world was changing so very fast and so was I. It seemed that I was now being prepared for another chapter to unfold in my life, and soon I would no longer sit underneath the bridge except to reminisce about past times and have some quiet space.

Much later, in 2018, my brother knocked down history. I was unaware of this until I arrived down in Ballybunion to discover that a lot of the cottage had been knocked down. The kitchen was gone altogether, but the bedrooms were left. The roof of the cottage was replaced with a flat felt roof and the cottage looked more like a shed. It was no longer Nan's castle or the place where we kids had lived our formative years. Some would say we just have to move on and embrace modern ways of living, but I hope we do not completely lose all of the quaint and beautiful little houses that we had back then.

Of all the angelic and elemental spirits I have encountered in my youth, one saintly being stands out from the rest. His name is Padre Pio. I have this very special monk—as well as a local priest—to thank for saving my life. One summer's day, when I was fourteen, I took myself down to Ballybunion Beach for a splashabout with two kids I was minding. One child belonged to the sweet shop owner who had given me a job, and the other was the daughter of a relative of the shop owner.

This was a regular occurrence because even though I could not swim I loved paddling in the beautiful waters of the Atlantic Ocean. That was a day I will remember as long as I live. On this particular afternoon, there were quite a few other people at the beach as well and some were swimming. While I was enjoying playing with the children, a chap I knew, who thought I could swim, suddenly pulled me under the water in play. It took him a couple of moments before he realised I couldn't swim and was in difficulties.

Before I knew it, I was dragged by a strong current away from the beach. The young man stood looking out at me, not knowing what to do. He could swim but not well enough to come and save me. In the meantime, I was in a terrible panic and no matter how hard I tried I couldn't get back to shore.

I was in real trouble when all at once I spotted Padre Pio coming towards me, floating over the water. At the time, I didn't know who he was. All I saw was a little old monk with holes in his hands and feet. He said: 'You'll be OK. All will be fine, don't panic.'

Then he vanished into thin air. The next thing I knew, it was all over. Somehow I was on the beach coughing and spluttering, spewing up seawater. A priest called Father Galvin had come and pulled me out of the sea and got me breathing again. I remember after regaining consciousness looking around in great urgency for the little kids I was minding, and being so relieved to see they were safe and well.

I believe God sent the holy monk, and this good priest that day to make sure I did not die. I had work to do, and if I was not sure of it then, I am definitely sure of it now. I know my friend meant no harm, but the harmless prank could easily have ended in tragedy.

By the time our family had got our new home, the seasons had turned nine times in my life, and the seasons were to turn another five times before I left home to make my own way in the world. As I moved from childhood to adulthood, I was greatly comforted to know that God, Padre Pio, Our Lady, to whom I have a real devotion, and the angels would always be there to help and support me through whatever obstacles would come my way.

Chapter 5
Injustice

At age thirteen, I left school. That was not unusual back then in Ireland. In those days, many young people started work at a relatively tender age. I said goodbye to the little school in Lisselton, and left the memories, good and bad, behind me. I had been released.

No more teachers, no more control. I was ready for adventure, life and freedom. I did learn to read and write at school, but I wasn't academic. Schools back then didn't have career counsellors and didn't go out of their way to nurture students' natural talents. I'm sure teachers did their best with what they knew at the time, and I do appreciate the bit of education I got, but I was still relieved to be out of the gap and able to start living.

As I headed out into the world, I was like a cork bobbing up and down on the water, happy to let life's journey take me where it would. I was going to go with the flow and see what happened. Mum, like all good parents, tried to stop me from giving up school, but I was determined to leave. She knew she could not win this one. I even burned all my books, celebrating as each one burned brightly in the range. Letting go of my schooldays was easy; no more would the smell of the wooden desks and the chairs fill my nostrils.

In later years, I worked really hard so that my kids got a better education than I did. But at the end of the day, there is no point in forcing a child to do what they really don't want to do, as it might well result in a disruptive child because they could feel trapped and frustrated. In my quieter moments, I wonder what would have happened if I stayed at school and studied, but in truth, it is all water under the bridge. If there is anything I can say to someone who may be faced with a life-changing decision, it is to follow your heart and let your spirit be your guide. You must be sure your decision is not just a fad, and it is something you really want to do.

I did *not* want to stay in school, and I know I made the right choice to leave. But there were things I didn't yet know about the new world I was stepping into. I thought that now I could do what I wanted, be who I wanted to be and could make my own choices about things all of the time. Of course, now I realise life is not like that, and you often exchange one level of control for another.

You first need to work to survive and then over time you may have a family and need to support them and pay a mortgage and school fees and so on. Some people would say that schooldays were the best days of your life. I didn't find that. But my childhood was not all bad, and I still sometimes crave the time of little tea parties under the bridge, my chats with my fairy friends, and my adventures with my donkey.

I believed that if I didn't get a job quickly, there was a chance Mum could somehow put me back in school. So without delay, I got a job as a hairdresser in a salon in Ballybunion, and I have to say I loved it. Like many Irish people, I enjoy meeting and talking with anyone and everyone, and there is nowhere better to have a chat than at a hairdressing salon. Before long, I was well-known to a lot of the locals in the area. I was chatty and friendly and that made me popular with the locals.

Many of the ladies who came to the salon could themselves talk for Ireland. They were real characters and would have you in fits of laughter as they chatted about what was going on in the area. They were great fun and so full of stories and gossip they were nearly better than the local newspapers!

That job didn't last long, though, as the owner had to move to a different town. We were good friends, and she was a real pet. Typical of the person she was, before she left she got me a job with another local hairdresser. My new employer was great craic, always up for a laugh and another joy to work for. However, my career was to come to a quick halt again as this owner said she had to close her shop as well.

Like the other hairdresser, she too was going to another town but asked if I would like to go with her. Unfortunately, this was not possible as it was too far away to walk to and public transport to the town was unpredictable. But I didn't have to wait too long for my next job. My aunt, who was employed in a hotel in Ballybunion, put in a good word for me and soon I was working there as a general dogsbody.

I had already heard of rite-of-passage pranks that are often played on new employees by more senior staff who think this is great fun. Examples would be the carpenter who sends the young apprentice for a loan of a glass hammer from the mechanic down the road, or the shopkeeper who sends the new lad to another shop owner to borrow the long stand—and he is left standing there for a long time! To be honest, I have no problems with these kinds of innocuous pranks, but the tricks played on me in my new job weren't that good-natured because some of the senior staff in the hotel were right bullies and liked to push me around, making me feel stupid. The fact that I was related to my aunt didn't protect me or stop some of the staff from trying to show how much of a fool I was in falling for their bad jokes and showing my innocence and inexperience at the same time.

It was just my luck to start working in the hotel during Listowel race week, one of the busiest times of the year in Ballybunion and the surrounding area. As the hotel was full of tourists, I was run off my feet, and there were lots of opportunities for the mean staff members to tease me and humiliate me. After putting up with these people for several weeks, I eventually couldn't take it anymore and resigned. I found out that employers could get away with a lot back then, and often did not pay menial staff like me what they were due. It was only because I was learning to stand up for myself at the time that I managed to get properly paid for the work I had done up to that point.

After that job, I worked in the sweet shop mentioned in the previous chapter. The owners were a married couple and the female owner became a really good friend. She was very kind and taught me many things, including how to cook, something I had not been interested in while living at home. She asked me if I would look after her young daughter at times, and I found it was a delight to take on this responsibility. I would often go on walks with the little one and sometimes her cousin, another little girl, would come along too. It was these two children with whom I walked on Ballybunion Beach the day I nearly drowned.

The next job I had after the sweet shop was as an assistant in a chemist's shop. My employers were again a married couple, and they had three children. I did some light housework for the couple as well. The owners and staff there were as supportive and loving as the staff in the hotel had been difficult and degrading. Like in my previous job, I was asked to do some childminding and frequently looked after their children.

I thoroughly enjoyed myself when I minded them. Between the kids and the adults, they were all wonderful, a great family. The experience I had there of people treating me with respect and care had a great part in restoring my faith in human nature after the painful experiences in the hotel.

I was by now having crushes on some boys and used to dream of having a family of my own one day. Some people said the man who got me would be very lucky as I wasn't a bad little *cook* and would make a good mother. Others said my future husband would want to watch out for flying pitchforks! When I noticed lads looking at me occasionally I would give demure glances back in their direction. Over time, I got to know some of them and enjoyed chatting away with them.

Gradually, I out-grew the shop and the childminding. My next port of call was a family pub. I was to work there for nearly a year and a half, and in this place, I was to undergo one of the scariest moments of my life. The family was well-liked and well-known in the area, and the couple who owned the pub were very good to me. They had three sons and a daughter, one of whom went to boarding school, a common practice for country children at that time in Ireland, while the other one worked in the pub with his parents.

I was a live-in staff member and worked at a number of jobs, more or less doing whatever was needed at any given time. I cleaned the rooms and also worked in the kitchen and the bar. The latter I especially liked as it involved dealing with and chatting with people, something I was good at. People liked my warmth and my smile. Being a little self-conscious, I would occasionally get a little embarrassed and go a little red when a customer said something like, 'Your smile is beautiful. It lights up your face, or, You bring sunshine into my day.'

In the time I worked there, it was rare that I got home to see my family. Work was constant and pubs in the country were open till very late. In those days, any worker was grateful to have a job and would work long hours for minimum wages. Back then it was almost a case of "anything goes" when it came to employers and their duties and responsibilities to their employees.

I suppose that is why we have far higher standards and legislation these days to protect those at work. I missed Mum and Dad at times, but I was happy to be able to help by giving them some money from my work. Things were often tight for them, and I know my parents appreciated my support.

My job there entailed a lot of hard work but that didn't bother me. My motto has always been 'An honest day's work for an honest day's pay.' No one could ever accuse me of being lazy or not committed to doing what needed to be done. The pub owners were the only ones who were allowed to handle money in the establishment, and this meant there could be no question of anyone being caught stealing. I was good at pulling pints, loved talking to the locals and very much enjoyed working in the place.

However, the energy changed when the son who attended boarding school came home for the summer holidays. This boy was made of different stuff than the rest of the family. He was often dishonest and a bit of a sleeveen. As bad as he was, his brother was the opposite, a lovely young lad who got on with his work and was really nice and kind to everyone.

The unpleasant brother took an interest in one of the girls who worked there, whom I was friends with, and kept following her around. She had no interest in him at all, and if you knew him, you'd understand why. He was a creep. One time this same lad told me to take money from the till, sign the book and bring it to him. I was a relative newbie at the time.

I knew the rules, but as he was the owner's son, I felt I had to do what I was told. A couple of days later he accused me of robbing, which was later proved by his father to be a lie. After that incident, his dad was very apologetic to me, which I was grateful for, and justifiably angry with his errant son. But this only made matters worse and resulted in the son being jealous of me, along with showing anger and resentment towards me. He was used to getting his own way by whatever means, fair or foul, and found it hard to take when things didn't work out in his favour.

He was somehow able to get passes for local dance halls and constantly pressurised several young female staff members to go out with him. He was turned down by them all as they knew what kind of person he was. But the person he harassed most was the girl I worked with. She kept rejecting his advances, and whenever he tried to kiss her, she pushed him away. Today, she would be able to take action against him and the workplace for sexual harassment, but in those days, women had little or no protection from bad behaviour of a sexual nature in workplaces, and their rights were not upheld the way they should have been.

In the dark recesses of his mind, the bad son hatched a plan, so he could do what he wanted to this girl, my colleague and friend. The owner of the pub and his wife headed out one night and left us in charge of running the pub together. The owners told my friend she could be in charge of taking the money that evening, as she was a senior staff member. We were very busy and the kind and honest son, who was quite the musician, helped entertain the guests by playing traditional tunes. As usual, there was always a lot to do, and as we came closer to the end of the evening, we noticed Mr Nasty was trying to play nice, and we wondered if he was up to something.

We always used to sit down to tea and biscuits at the end of a long night's work, which we considered a well-earned reward and break before bed. When it came to that time on this particular evening, to our surprise the bad son offered to make tea. He said it was a gesture of goodwill, so we could all become friends again. He was almost pleasant, and we found this a welcome change from his usual behaviour. He sat down with us, and we chatted for a bit.

Then he said he would make us another cup of tea if we wanted, and we said grand. By this time, we had decided to go up to our rooms, so he took the tea up to us. When he put the cups in front of us he told us not to switch teas, and then he said goodnight and left to go to his own room. Had we been less tired we would have noticed that was a strange thing to say about the cups. But we did swap them because I like a lot of milk in my tea and my friend liked it a little, and there was a lot of milk in the tea she had been given.

We continued talking for a short while as we finished our tea. We chatted about different things and then my friend brought up the nasty son. As I drained the last drop of my tea, she said she was suspicious because she didn't believe he had gone back to his room, as neither of us had heard him walking on the squeaky floorboard in the hall after he left us, something he could not have avoided doing. As I thought about what she said, I suddenly felt funny, and everything went out of shape. Then I was out of it, unconscious, comatose.

My friend filled me in as to what happened next. In the pandemonium that ensued, she ran downstairs for help. I never found out if the son was outside our room, but in the greater scheme of things, that didn't matter. Luckily, the owners had just returned from their night out. They came into the room and, seeing I was virtually unresponsive, managed to get me into my bed and phoned the doctor.

He came very quickly and after examining me said my heart seemed enlarged and was racing, and he was very worried about me. At that stage, I had partly regained consciousness and could understand what people were saying, but I couldn't move my body or talk at all. The doctor asked if I was taking drugs and the owner spoke on my behalf and said I wasn't.

The doctor then took my blood and said he wanted to get me into the hospital. But it was apparently full that night, no beds were available. So I lay there in a kind of coma, fighting for my life. I found out later that the doctor never received the results of the blood test, because they mysteriously went missing. When he visited the next day the doctor said there was not much he could do for me given he didn't know what I might have inadvertently taken. If he prescribed a particular medicine for me, it might adversely affect me and further endanger my life, so he waited and hoped I would recover.

After two weeks, I was no better. I wasn't fully here or fully there. I had no awareness of my physical body but did feel my spirit moving in and out of my body. When I was out of body I was able to float around the room and could see what was going on. Then the day came when the doctor thought I was near death, and he told the woman of the house to call for the priest. He said it was only a matter of time before I would die.

'Get her anointed and call her family,' he told the pub owner's wife. The woman went off in a daze to get the priest, but for some reason, my family wasn't called.

The doctor was a kind man. 'She is too young to die,' he said, after sitting with me for a few minutes, and started to pray in earnest for me. He said only God could help me at this stage and promised Him he would do anything He wanted if He would only let this young woman live.

Soon after he said those words the priest arrived. He came over to the bed, and looking at me said, 'This young lady was going nowhere. She still has a lot of work to do.'

Then two amazing things happened. I knew he knew I could hear him, and when he spoke those words, I started to feel my spirit re-enter my body. God had saved my life again. I opened my eyes to the great relief of everyone, and then I heard someone say, 'Don't talk about what happened to her in front of her. Let's go into the kitchen.'

As they got up to leave, the boy who had poisoned my tea suddenly burst into the room and apologised to me for what he had done. With a look of horror on her face, his mother shouted at him to shut up and leave the room. She actually pushed him out the door.

The family knew what they should have done after the son confessed to his crime, but they made the decision to protect him and not tell anyone what happened. It took a few days for me to fully come back to the real world and for my body to start moving properly again. The pub owners were so relieved their son had not killed me that I could have asked for the moon and got it. Later, my friend told me she had realised what had happened and was worried sick about me.

The owners and I talked, and I agreed not to tell the truth about what happened, as it would have destroyed the family. I now know I was being manipulated, and my youth and inexperience were used against me. It took me another couple of months to completely recover, and I felt like I was living in a prison all that time. I told the pub owners I was leaving at Christmas, and they said they understood and were really sorry for what had happened. What they said didn't matter to me because what they did was all wrong. They had covered up a crime to protect their son, and in so doing, they let him get away scot-free.

At his wife's funeral many years later, the pub owner came up to me and said, 'We did you very wrong.' They had. There was no denying the damage they did in covering up for what their son had done, as those events had done a lot of harm to me for a long time afterwards. It took away my trust and faith in people. Mentally and emotionally, I was scared.

As for the physical side of things, I cannot say if the drugs did lasting injury or not. I never had a full check-up after what happened, so I don't know exactly what damage was done to my body during that event. I also have no idea if the drugs given to me at that time had an influence on what happened to me later.

At the time, I was just grateful I had survived and couldn't wait to leave that place forever. If my ordeal had happened today, things would have been very different indeed. I would have stood up for myself and told the police everything.

VICTIM IMPACT STATEMENT

To the son of the publican who almost killed me

In your quest for you to have your own way with my co-worker, you tried to drug her. By happenstance, I took the drugs instead which nearly resulted in my death. The cover-up that happened afterwards to save you took away the integrity of your mother and father. They did not stand up for what was right. They should have.

I will never forgive you for what you did. I placed myself in your family's care, and this was what I got. I have never received justice and realise I will not now. I believe and hope that God will make you answer for what you've done.

Here and now, I am giving a voice to my sixteen-year-old self, and the opportunity to put on record your crime against me.

This was the second time I was placed in the jaws of death, and the second time divine mercy and prayer brought me back because I had work to do. Although I am glad God saved my life, the betrayal and abandonment surrounding what I saw as attempted murder scarred me for many years afterwards.

Chapter 6
Darkness and Light

One night I fell asleep and had a dream. I was a child again, and it was a gorgeous sunny day before any darkness entered my life. I could see the happiness and joy radiating from me. I had just eaten berries from the orchard and then I went and played with my beloved donkey, once again riding through the fields, a little girl on a mission to God knows where doing God knows what.

After that adventure, I went for a swing at the farm gate with my friend. "Swing the Gate" had to be played by two children. One child would stand on the gate and the other would open it. Then the second child would push the gate forward, jump up beside their friend, and the gate would swing shut with a great big thump. It was fantastic fun, and myself and my friend would do it over and over again.

In the dream, I could still hear our screams of delight, echoes from the past. But the clash, bang and wallop of the gate closing would really annoy my mother, Nan and big sister, and they would tell us to stop. I often had a problem with people telling me what to do, so when this happened I would encourage my friend to keep on playing.

We were having so much fun, swinging gaily backwards and forwards until one of the meanies came out and gave out to us. In this instance, it was my older sister. She had a red angry face on her and shouted at us to get off the gate. My friend and I ran off through the muck in our wellies and through the gathering of hens, who squawked loudly as they scattered out of the way.

But when I turned to talk to my comrade-in-arms, she was gone, and the dream shifted to a day when the gate was closed, and I looked very forlorn. I climbed up on the gate and hung over it in sadness. I was all alone, with tears rolling down my cheeks. My inner child was crying out for someone to play with her and love her, for someone to see her and listen to her.

The world no longer seemed like a good place to be in. I was miserable and isolated and felt like my childhood had prematurely come to an end. Then the dream changed once more, and I was running in the fields again, but this time, as the adult me and I were running with the child me and protecting her. I had become her best friend. How amazing that was! And once more I was integrated and whole.

When I woke up I lay there, thinking about the dream. I realised it showed me that even though I had gone through some very difficult times, my adult self could now be there for my younger self, and my child could be healed. As well as helping her heal, she could open a door to where she could recall good times that had been forgotten. As a result, of all the pain, I knew the sun would shine again. From that day on I promised I would be there for my inner child and would make sure she was safe and always protected.

When I was young there were times when I thought I was a bad child, but I know now that I wasn't. I was just lost and hurt. When I felt unjustly treated I got angry and sometimes aggressive, which was my way of defending myself. My older sister, who often pushed my buttons, seemed to get on better with Mum and Nan than I did, and in my eyes, they gave her preferential treatment. Where Nan could be hurtful to me, she seemed to dote on my sister.

She often bought sweets for her and always took her side in any argument. Whether she was right or wrong didn't matter. One day, in my temper, I threw an iron bar at my sister and only for the intervention of my dad telling her to duck, it would have hit her. On another day, I caught Mum's toe with a pitchfork.

In fairness, I didn't mean to, but you know how it is. In a real rage, you don't see what you are doing. You act first before you think of what the consequences could be.

It was only years later when I started working on myself that I realised how violated I was. As I came to an understanding of my anger, I was able to see why it was there and realised it wasn't my fault. The only awareness I have of abuse as a very small child was when I overheard Mum talking to Dad about what the hospital doctor had told her: that my kidney infections were possibly a result of being interfered with. But as I grew up I distinctly remembered instances of sexual abuse from a number of men. One individual in particular looms large in those memories.

He was a close member of my extended family, and he abused me since early childhood. He was evil personified, with no respect for me as a child or care for the damage he was doing. This person was supposed to look after me and protect me. I hope that if he reads this, he knows God's judgement is awaiting him on the other side. I cannot forgive him, not yet anyway.

My pain is still too raw, and forgiveness for him is not high on my list of priorities. It is only to protect my family and extended family that I have not named him here. I have no doubt that if he reads this book he will know I am talking about him.

There were lots of times during my childhood he touched me inappropriately and tried to get me to do things that were wrong. Some memories stand out more than others. When I was a teenager, he grabbed me and tried to push my head between his legs, demanding oral sex. He probably had done this many times before, but I have blocked those memories out. Maybe I remember this incident more than the other times because I had grown strong enough by then and was able to fight back, and refused to do what he wanted.

Later, when I was engaged to be married, the same man threatened me with a gun and tried to get me to have sex with him. He said, 'If I can't get you, then no one will.' When I faced this man down, I knew he was a coward at heart. I didn't care if he had a gun or not—he was no longer able to control me, this horrible man who had blighted my life for so many years. Dismissively, I just turned around and walked away. In the end, he was powerless, and I was now free.

What a vile person he was. He should have gone to prison for a long time. I didn't realise how many memories I had suppressed until I started writing about my near-drowning experience and being poisoned by the pub owner's son. Something clicked in my mind and several forgotten memories began to resurface.

Some were of sexual abuse and others were emotional abuse, but I have to say I really was shocked at the level of damage that had actually been done to me. In saying that, I am aware that I still only remember a portion of those terrible events, and maybe that is a good thing because what I recall may be sufficient to deal with at the moment.

I have other abusive and uncomfortable childhood memories which are still part of my untold story, but I feel the level of disclosure I have given here is enough. In remembering my history, I think of other children who have been abused as well, and the depth of damage that has been done to them. I implore parents to be aware and look out for predators, and take notice if a child's behaviour suddenly changes or disimproves. Sometimes bad people hide in the shadows of our own lives, wolves in sheep's clothing.

I am proud of how resilient I have been. I could have gone down the road of resentment and bitterness after all the things that happened to me, and I doubt anyone could blame me if I did, but I am glad I still carry a great deal of love in my heart. I have no doubt that my unwavering connection to my faith greatly helped me hold onto my light. I have a strong love for Our Lady as well as Padre Pio and am grateful for the assistance and comfort they brought me over the years. I also believe they will guide my path to the end of my life.

I still think it's strange that Mum and others in the family accepted that Dad was intuitive and sensitive but couldn't accept that I was, and they tried to hide or block the gifts I had. Dad, though, did respect my intuitive side because he felt I had probably inherited it from him. My dad was a gentle Irish farmer who always showed great respect to the animals, to the land, to nature and the elemental kingdom. He upheld the ancient custodian traditions of the land and saw its protection and care as a sacred trust placed in his hands.

Whenever I was with him at festivals and harvests, I noticed he always took time to give gratitude for the earth and what it produced. I can also still see him cycling up to the house after a long day's work and then breaking a beaming smile when he saw us. I always remember being delighted when I'd spot him and announce, 'Daddy's home!' To this day, I cherish those special times.

I missed him when I went away to work. Over the following years, I visited home as often as I could, but it was never long enough. There were always those at home who welcomed me with open arms when I took short breaks from work, but also those who were delighted to see me go back to work again! But I am sure that is normal in any family. My brothers and sisters were growing up and the turning seasons brought constant change to our little home under Cnoc an Óir.

It's interesting, as a child you can't wait to grow up and be in charge of your own life, and you don't see old Father Time catching up on your parents. Even though you may lose friends and relations from time to time, you still don't connect their deaths to the losses you will inevitably have of those closest to you. It's in looking back you realise how precious those times were.

After I left the pub, I was lucky to get employed again by the people I had worked for before in the sweet shop. Thankfully, the work there wasn't too demanding as my concentration at the time was not good. I have no doubt this was the result of the drugs that nearly killed me on that fateful night, and it was a considerable length of time before those lingering effects finally wore off. I wasn't going to remain in the shop for long, but it offered me a safe haven with wonderful people I trusted.

Chapter 7
A Happy Time, a Turbulent Time

After the painful experiences in the pub, I have to say working in the shop again was a lifesaver and gave me a chance to rebuild my self-confidence and self-belief. In the morning, I cleaned the house for the family, and in the afternoon, I served customers in the sweet shop.

The woman who had been so supportive of me in the past came through when I needed her most. I will always remember her for that. As well as serving in the shop, I was minding her two children.

By now, her family had expanded a bit with the birth of a baby boy. I was delighted as it was fun to be in the children's bright and bubbly company. It was certainly hard to stay depressed around children. They really are magical and reminded me of what it was like to play and laugh.

There was always a lot to do and the work with the family was varied, so I never got bored. I needed gentleness and care after the job in the pub and count myself really fortunate to have worked for this couple. They were caring and kind, way beyond what they needed to be as employers. Over the two periods I was employed by them, I grew a lot and our connections became stronger. I am very grateful for the profoundly positive effect they had on my life which helped to ease a lot of my pain of the past.

I was now approaching my late teens and resumed socialising with some of the girls and guys I used to hang around with when I previously worked in the area. When I was in their company I learned to hide my lack of self-esteem by talking a lot. Someone once said I could talk the hind legs off a donkey, and I learned to laugh with the lads as though I was one of them. I could set boundaries too, and no one was allowed to take liberties.

A young man went to lift my dress up one day and a swift knee in a sensitive place had him singing falsetto for a while. He never tried that again and later apologised for his behaviour. We made peace with each other and moved on. I knew at heart he was a decent skin, and not like the sinister characters I encountered earlier in life.

During this time, an important event happened in my life. While I was working in the shop one day I met a handsome young man, Tony. We were attracted to each other straight away, and it wasn't long before he asked me out. It mightn't have seemed an ideal pairing as Tony is a man of few words whereas I can talk for Ireland. However, we just matched each other really well and understood each other.

I found out he was of UK origin and a carpenter and heaven help us, he actually played cricket. Just imagine what my Irish ancestors would have thought of that! In a place where football is king and GAA is God, trust me to meet an English cricket player, which in Kerry is a very rare occurrence indeed.

Ballybunion is known as a great seaside resort, and for Tony and me, there was never a shortage of places to go and things to see, especially in the summertime when the tourist season was in full swing. Sometimes we went to the cinema, and other times we used to go roller skating in the Atlantic Skating Rink. I was not exactly a graceful swan—more like Bambi on ice, and I envied Tony's natural ability to skate around the ring like a god. Well, he thought he was anyway. In truth, he just didn't fall down as much as I did!

But even if he was kind of OK at skating, I was a far better dancer. I could really get down and boogie when we danced along to the popular groups at the time. A lot of well-known Irish bands, groups and singers came to play in Ballybunion, and we were lucky to enjoy the sounds of Thin Lizzy (with the very cool Phil Lynott), the dulcet tones of Dickie Rock who was the sex symbol of his time, and the great balladeer and Beatles lookalike Johnny McEvoy. Then there was everybody's favourite, the country, traditional and easy-listening singer, Big Tom. Tony and I danced and laughed and sang our hearts out to these great entertainers and so many more too.

Then there were times when Tony and I just strolled around the town, hanging out and simply enjoying each other's company. Over time, it became clear that we had something very special. Holding hands with Tony as we walked along the beach in the moonlight is just one of the lovely romantic moments I remember.

After a while, I felt we should get married. To be honest, it was pretty much a mutual agreement. Tony quipped that he wanted a prenuptial agreement to protect his cricket bat, gloves, pads and cricket ball, and I agreed we should have no problem with that at all.

We were married in the little church in Ballybunion in 1987. What a wonderful day my wedding day was, one of the happiest moments of my life. I also felt very blessed that it was also a Marian year. Now, Tony and I were one. I never thought I could be that happy or that much in love.

After the ceremony, we got some photographs taken on Ballybunion Beach and then we slowly wound our way in a convoy of cars to the reception in the Earl of Desmond Hotel in Tralee. There were crowds of people around, not only because we had invited lots of guests to the wedding but also because the Fleadh Cheoil, an annual celebration of Irish music and dance, was being held there that week. Listowel is a town located between Ballybunion and Tralee. Of course, it would not have been my wedding without a spot of drama! As we were inching our way through Listowel, our convoy inadvertently adding to the bedlam of the busy town, the wedding car crashed into the car in front. It happened just as my little brother and niece were throwing flowers out the window of the wedding car at passersby.

Thankfully, there was little damage done and our wedding party continued on to the reception. People in Kerry are warm-hearted, and to this day, I remember the locals in Listowel waving and smiling at the children as they threw the flowers around with gay abandon.

After our wedding, we moved into a house in Ballybunion which was owned by Tony's father, my new father-in-law. Within a few months, I was pregnant. I was so excited. We had a baby on the way! Taking into account the fact that I had so much trauma and stress with my reproductive organs and my stomach, it was both a miracle and a relief to be pregnant because I had always wanted children. However, even though my heart was full of joy and celebration, I was also quite worried and fearful about how the pregnancy would go.

I went to my GP to confirm my pregnancy and to check I was OK, and he said everything looked fine. Back in my day it was the GP took the lead role until it was time to give birth, or if there was a problem. How the world has changed from the time of *Call the Midwife* and home births and a good local doctor, to today where women go for regular visits to obstetricians and get ultrasound scans to see how their baby is developing.

Midway through my pregnancy, I began feeling some pains and aches, which I just took as being par for the course for a woman carrying a child. When I was five and a half months pregnant I went out for the evening with Tony. It was race week in Listowel, and as I knew the atmosphere would be electric, I was really looking forward to being out walking among the crowd and soaking up the energy of the happy upbeat community. The crescendo of noise was added to by music being played on the streets and in the pubs. I hadn't been able to join in the fun and excitement of the event for a few years previously because I had always been working elsewhere whenever race week was on. Because of this, I was all the more determined not to miss out this time.

Then, out of the blue, I started to feel unwell and decided to sit down for a bit. But instead of feeling better I just felt worse and worse. Eventually, I had to tell Tony I had to go home. By the time I arrived back at the house, I felt really ill and had started bleeding. We rang my GP, and he told me to go straight to the hospital. It was clear from the doctor's sense of urgency that I was having a real problem.

By now, I was bleeding heavily and was in a lot of pain. I was also very distressed and fearful.

I have to say the nurse who first attended me when I got to Tralee General Hospital was great. She got a wheelchair for me and put me in a bed in a ward. Before long, a doctor came. He was an obstetrician.

After a quick examination, he told me I was in labour. I can't remember whether I was sedated or if I passed out, but I don't recall the entire labour and the birth of the baby. When I came to they told me I had lost my child. I was so distraught I started crying great sobs of grief. I felt my heart just broke at this tragic news.

Then, as if that wasn't bad enough, the obstetrician who was supposed to look after me and suddenly gave me a hard smack across my face. He hit me so hard I will never forget the shock, pain and hurt of that blow. Instead of receiving compassion and understanding, I got cruelty from a man whom I feel was a bully, and who had issues with women. He was supposed to be an obstetrician who cared for pregnant ladies. In my opinion, he was in the wrong job. My GP later said, when he saw the bruise on my face, I must have been hit really hard.

Neither the doctor nor the nurse in attendance told me what they did with my baby, and to this day, I have not been able to find out exactly what happened. When I recovered I searched for my medical records, but they seemed to have just vanished into thin air. Believe it or not, the doctor actually told me we would never find the file. With the way he treated me, I would not be surprised if he hadn't got rid of them himself. It is actually only in relatively recent legislation that people have become entitled to their own medical records.

Up to date, the obstetrician was right, no records were found anywhere. The whole miscarriage was like a non-event like it never happened. There was also no record of the doctor hitting me. Today that would be seen as assault and the doctor would have to face the consequences of his actions. It left me with a very uncomfortable feeling of a cover-up.

The one thing I did discover was that the baby was a little boy, and I named him Michael, after my favourite archangel. It is hard to believe women were treated like that in those days, and that the lost babies were just disposed of. And yes, that was what happened to a lot of them back then.

When I was ready to be discharged no one in the hospital came to talk to me about how I could help myself deal with the loss of my child. I was left to bear the grief and suffering on my own. There was also no counselling or aftercare service available to me. I hear it is much different now, thank God because I would not want anyone to go through what I did.

I was abandoned mentally, emotionally and physically by the hospital, and I was in an awful state when I got home. I was not able to function. All I could do was sleep and hope I would never wake up. All my dreams of having a child were shattered and the conspiracy of silence that surrounded the event left me absolutely bereft.

My GP was genuinely upset when he heard what had happened to me in the hospital, and came to visit me as soon as he could. This man, an ordinary doctor, worked so hard to help me heal. I told him how bad I felt and that I was too weak to stand. When he checked the medication I had been put on, he told me I had been taking too much Valium. At the time, it was the drug of choice for some doctors. Nowadays, we are questioning the wisdom of overprescribing meds, as doctors today realise the consequences of such actions.

I owe my mental health, if not my life, to this kind of doctor who worked tirelessly to bring me back to normality. Every day for a number of weeks he came to see me, and bit by bit my emotional and mental health improved. He was just an amazing person. He kept a close eye on my medication, very gradually reducing the doses. He was afraid that if I came off them too quickly my body might go into shock. He showed tremendous care, professionalism and humanity, a man who truly honoured his oath to care for people.

I was grateful to get support from four other unexpected heroes as well. The first was my mother-in-law, Nora, and she showed me what it was like to be really there for someone. When I could not get out of bed, she looked after me like I was her own daughter.

She made special meals for me and stood over me while I ate them. 'Come on dear, eat up, you need your strength,' she'd say. She nursed me back to health, bit by bit. During those dark days, there were moments when I found it hard to care about anything, but Mum-in-law had a way of getting through to me.

After a period of gentle care, Nora saw a little tough love was in order. She became a bit of a sergeant major and got me up and made me walk around the place, a little at first, and then more and more each day. I was in real pain and afraid to move around too much in case I damaged myself.

She was aware of this and knew I needed time to regain my confidence. It was around this time I developed a love of television soaps. If I was good and did my exercises, Nora allowed me to watch them. Her rules and regulations actually gave me a bit of discipline, and I knew she had my best interests at heart.

Then the shop owners who re-employed me after the pub ordeal heard my news. I have to say they couldn't have been kinder to me. They kept in close contact all through the aftermath and the recovery from the miscarriage, and I really did feel I had an extra family looking after me. My last lovely hero was the girl who had done my wedding makeup for me as a gift. She too, stepped up and was there for me as I healed in mind and body. I will never forget the compassion these people showed me out of the goodness of their hearts.

It took a long time for the slap the doctor gave me in the hospital to heal fully, and the emotional pain lasted much longer than the bruise. He never took responsibility for what he had done. The medical profession rarely did back then. Some of them had the attitude that we knew nothing and that they were gods. I am glad that somewhere along the way at least some of them have discovered they are not gods and also that women are now a little better protected from the arrogance of the time.

I don't know what that man had against me. Now I know it wasn't me, it was him. By chance, one day, I met him in the street. I stopped to ask him why he hit me and what had happened to my child. His reply said it all.

'Women like you should never get pregnant,' he declared.

When he spoke those words I lost the plot. I shouted at him as he walked away, 'God will judge you for what you did!'

This particular doctor was a middle-aged man, and he lived in Tralee. He took the Hippocratic Oath to take care of his patients, and he violated this precious promise. The law is different now, and there is more accountability but back then these self-absorbed people were above the law. They did what they wanted and got away with just about anything. Anyone who spoke out about injustices done to them by these physicians was like a voice crying in the wilderness.

It was difficult enough to have your heart crushed by the loss of a baby, but not to have clarity and closure as well made matters so much worse. In those days, there was no understanding or compassion for the mothers and fathers of these little ones. Even in hospitals where religion was a powerful force at the time, the medical world was a dictatorship and empathy and kindness were in short supply. I must add that this didn't extend to some of the nurses, who were kind, caring and sensitive but wouldn't have been listened to at the time. Those who dared to speak out would have found themselves ostracised.

You would wonder how certain people, who proclaimed so loudly that a foetus was a child and a gift from God, could also treat miscarried and stillborn babies so badly. It is only in relatively recent years that maternity hospitals have changed their policy in looking after these poor infants and are now showing respect for the little souls that did not quite make it here. They also have more understanding of the grieving mothers and their broken hopes and dreams. Most of those in charge of health care have retrospectively acknowledged that the way women and their lost children were treated was very wrong. It is ironic that as religious orders lose their grip on the nation our country is becoming more Christian, more accepting and inclusive. Imagine!

I often comfort myself by thinking my baby might be buried in the little angels' plot in Tralee graveyard, but one thing I do know for sure is that wherever he is, he is resting in peace.

Today, I would have no hesitation in getting that doctor barred as a medical practitioner for life for what he did to me, and I am sure to other women too. This conspiracy of silence did great damage to women and allowed these nefarious practices to continue for far too long. The hurt that these people caused was enormous and women are still suffering the effects of their actions today. There are so many with physical trauma, others with mental health issues and more in deep emotional pain.

Two years after that saga, while I was still grieving, I got pregnant again. As you can imagine, I was excited but terrified. I was afraid not only of losing this baby but also of having to go through a repeat of what happened in the hospital with Michael. My stress was enormous, but it is amazing how different the experience was with a different doctor. The obstetrician I had while I was pregnant with my son James could not have been nicer, nor could he have cared for me better.

Dr Creedon, a man with a fair collection of children of his own was there for me, not just as a doctor, but as a human being. He spent hours talking to me and listened to all my fears and worries. As a result, he had a really calming influence on me. At one point, he asked me if I had ever taken an overdose of drugs, even by accident. At the time, I believed he thought I might have tried to commit suicide, and I emphatically assured him that I hadn't.

It was only a couple of days later that I remembered the poisoning in the pub, and then more recently being put on excessively high medication after the miscarriage. It is amazing how effectively the mind can cause us to block and forget bad memories, pain and trauma. I rang Dr Creedon and filled him in. He was shocked by what I told him, but the information joined the dots for him regarding my physical and mental state. With no access to medical records in the hospital and the fact that the poisoning was covered up by the family, I really was the only one who could truly bear witness to those times.

I now believe the second pregnancy kicked my body into its cellular memory of the previous events. Finding the fear, worry and stress too great, my body went into complete shock from time to time. I spent a lot of the pregnancy resting in the hospital because Dr Creedon didn't want to take any chances with the health of the baby or myself. Anyway, as bad as the other doctor was, this doctor was excellent. He did tell me daunting news, however.

He said that after assessing me, he said I had a lot of damage done to my insides. He also told me I was too dry and that every time I got pregnant I would be putting my life at risk. I sometimes felt I didn't help matters either as I suffered from coeliac disease and ate a lot of the wrong types of food. As a result, I had to be checked regularly on a heart monitor machine, because that is one of the areas which can be affected by the disease.

One weekend Dr Creedon let me home, just for a few hours. He thought a change of scene might do me good, rather than have me cooped up in a hospital bed all the time.

'You will have to come back in straight away if anything changes,' he told me.

Thank God, freedom, I thought. But as soon as I was at the door of my house, I started bleeding. Frightened, I went immediately back into the hospital, and the bleeding stopped a little while later. We tried the same thing—release on parole—a few weeks later. But I started bleeding again, and it was back to the hospital once more.

During the pregnancy, I didn't watch much TV but definitely was an avid fan of *Coronation Street.* I wouldn't miss it and when the intro tune to the series came on my little unborn baby always became very relaxed. He seemed to love the music, and sensing this made me feel more relaxed as well. My dear mother-in-law, Nora, had passed away some months back, and I frequently sensed her around during the pregnancy.

It was a great blessing to know she was supporting me from the other side. Another thing that gave me great comfort was that I was sure she was taking care of my little angel, Michael, in heaven. I also had a strong intuition that the two of them were really connected.

The way Dr Creedon treated me gave me real confidence. When he said, nearer the birth, 'I am not going to lose you or this child, not on my watch.' I knew he meant it. James' due date was the 14th of March 1992, which I took to be a sign from the heavens. Nora had passed away on the 10th of March the previous year and was buried on the 14th of March. Because of the alignment of these two dates, I just knew he was going to be alright, that his granny would look after him and me.

'We will be fine,' I said to my doctor. 'Angels are watching over us.'

James actually stayed in my belly until the 22nd of March. He is a bit chilled by nature, so it is not surprising that he took his time before making his grand entrance. The actual labour was short, only about half an hour, which was a huge relief after the months of fear and worry I went through. When James was ready, he came out like a rocket. Thank God and His Blessed Mother that in the end, the birth turned out to be stress-free.

No one could imagine how happy I felt when I held little James in my arms for the first time. He was beautiful and such a laid-back baby, and I cried many tears of joy. It had all been worth it, and I was so grateful. Tony was so proud too: he had a son! Even Dr Creedon looked like the cat that got the cream. It certainly had been a team effort.

James was perfect in every way. This experience was such a contrast from the first pregnancy, and I was so ecstatic with this wonderful new miracle in my life. He was a very quiet and gentle little baby with a great temperament, so easy to mind, and everyone wanted to hold him. He was also really affectionate.

I knew that my mother-in-law had helped in spirit during the birth because I actually saw her standing at the end of my hospital bed. I felt her energy holding me in love. I am so grateful for the special gifts she gave me: for her son as my husband, her support before and after her passing, and for minding my little Michael in heaven.

From the start, my gran doted on James and really loved the fact that he was born so close to her own birthday, the 20th of March. She always insisted on celebrating her birthday with her great-grandson, and she never missed his big day as long as she was alive. It was lovely she took such an interest in him, but she was a great woman. By that stage, I had long forgiven her for burning Nan's stuff after she died all those years ago. My own mum was also delighted to see James whenever we visited the family home.

Another wonderful thing was that after James was born, I had no depression, no illness and no postnatal trauma. Nothing. I was in great form and would walk everywhere, showing off my son to the world. I used to do an eight-mile circuit walk around the locality, and I was able to do it without a problem in the world. I was really high on life.

I also used to take James down to the beach, the same place my mum took me and my sister when we were small. It was amazing to see him playing on the sand just like I had done as a child and to know he was mine. He would always get loads of oohs and aahs when people came up to look at him—my baby—and congratulate me. I realised what a gift it was to be a mum and how much you can love your child.

Over the years, quite a few members of my family have been born or died under the sign of Pisces, the fish. James's daughter, my granddaughter, was born on the 8th of March, Nan's death was on the 14th, Gran's birthday is on the 20th, and James's birthday is on the 22nd.

Even though I was just a little whip of a thing at eight stone when I had James, I felt so alive and had no shortage of energy. It was wonderful to be able to celebrate my new baby, and I was so thankful to the kind and caring doctor who helped make the whole pregnancy and birth so manageable and trouble-free.

Chapter 8
JD's Pub

In contrast to the turmoil surrounding the pregnancies in my personal life, my work life at this stage was stable and fulfilling. I really liked working in the sweet shop. My employers were exceptional individuals and had a wonderfully positive effect on me and my life generally, but I knew I wouldn't be staying there forever.

After a few years working for them, I wanted to move on and work in the pub environment again. My bad experience in the other pub didn't affect the good memories I had of being a barmaid there. I liked the environment and the punters, the laughter and the fun. Nothing beats the atmosphere of an Irish public house that's full of people enjoying a relaxing drink, telling stories, singing songs and listening to music.

I applied to a few places and was delighted when I found employment at JD's, a pub located towards the middle of the main street. You could often smell the sea when the salty scent wafted in on breezy days. The pub also had a beer garden where people could smoke while having a drink and a chat.

Our town is a really popular place for tourists, especially in the summer, and so the pubs are always sure to have a lot of customers. I was lucky to have been employed in one of the most popular establishments in the town in which there was also regular music and entertainment.

I love being around people, and in JD's, there were always a lot of visitors coming and going every day. We got travellers from all over the world and all walks of life, and it would never be long before tourists were chatting away with locals. They loved listening to the tales of the wise old men of the local area who would sup their pints and enjoy telling tales of other days. During the winter, even though it was quieter with the tourists gone home, it was still pretty lively as it was a popular haunt for local people to meet, a real hub for the community. The pub was traditional in appearance, had character and gave its customers a sense of what Ireland was like in bygone days.

It had an interior thatched roof which hung like an awning over the bar and even though the thatch was imitation it still looked pretty authentic. Wooden beams were in the ceiling and throughout the pub there was comfortable seating. The atmosphere was heightened by its decor: fishing nets draped across the ceiling and postcards collaged on the walls which had been sent by those who had visited the place. If you like, they were leaving something behind to show they had passed this way. The back wall of the pub was completely covered with different kinds of bottles, and the bar itself was a half-moon shape, which was a little unusual but actually blended in well with the overall warmth and welcoming atmosphere of the pub.

I tremendously enjoyed my time there, all seventeen years of it. I can still hear the clink of glasses, the laughter and the banter of all the customers. It was such great craic. JD's became like my family, a home from home, and before long,

I was a regular fixture in the bar, pulling pints and serving the lovely lunatics who frequented the place. They gave me just as much entertainment as I gave them.

Some people were really funny, even without being aware of it themselves. Sometimes they told tales in a way that would have you in kinks and other times they reminisced about the past, telling stories of their adventures. I love laughter and joy and warmth, and those emotions were there in abundance. The happy atmosphere in the pub made it a place that uplifted anyone who visited. It was like you were almost guaranteed a giggle just by coming in the doors.

I loved my job so much that it never felt like work. Bands often came to play, and we also had regular Irish traditional music sessions. The bands usually performed at weekends and were positioned near the front bar where I was stationed, which was fantastic. They only took short breaks—a quick drink, a bag of crisps—and then would resume rocking the house because they wanted to keep the party going. Then on the nights when there was no band, we had a great DJ who would spin the sort of tunes that would have you tapping your feet or dancing around the tables. The place being as lively as it was, it would never be long before everyone would join in on a good old sing-song, which would make closing time quite fluid.

The owner of the pub and my boss, Sean, was a bit of a *seanchai* or Irish storyteller, and he would regale the punters with stories that had been handed down from generation to generation. As well as that, Sean enjoyed spinning his own yarns and the customers loved listening to him. He had a real talent for holding people in the palm of his hand as he told them tall tales from the olden days. It was like they were spellbound. 'And that was the absolute gospel truth,' he would say at the end of a story, with a nudge and a wink and a very broad smile. Some of us were in no doubt that he had kissed the Blamey Stone.

Sean often got me to drive to the wholesaler's in my little car to collect drinks for the bar. I would usually ring ahead, so there would be no delays. For sure, we couldn't have customers waiting for their drinks! I was only a learner driver then and was a little nervous carrying all the supplies from the wholesaler's. As I had to fill the car up so much, I nearly couldn't see around me, I had to drive at a snail's pace all the way back to the pub.

The good thing was, there weren't as many police around back then as there are now. These days I might have been cautioned about overloading my vehicle, but back then, even if I did meet some guards while ferrying all the stock, more than likely they would end up helping me to unload the beer and spirits back at the pub. They were gentlemen and would not see a damsel in distress—or a drought in the local pub! Of course, they would never partake in the drink themselves. The guards and the priests were all teetotallers in those days, and if they did take a drop, it was purely for medicinal purposes.

Now and again motorbike gangs came to visit. As befitted their status, they were always dressed in their typical gear, leathers and denim, and most of them were bearded. They were jesters and jokers and when they were in town the craic was mighty. With a few drinks, some of them would get a bit rowdy, but I could always give as good as I got and peace would usually be rapidly restored. In truth, they were just a bunch of guys who occasionally let off steam, and behind all their macho bravado they were decent lads.

If any of their own really stepped out of line, they sorted things out themselves. I love music and whenever I wasn't serving or nattering to the customers I would sing along to the tunes playing in the background, happy out in my world. If the bikers were in the bar, now and again one of them would creep up on me from behind and serenade me with songs like "The Rose of Tralee" or "When Irish Eyes are Smiling". Some of the lads had great voices, and they always made me laugh when they sang to me. I might have occasionally blushed a little, because I was a bit shy, but I did enjoy the attention. It was all good-natured fun.

In those years, closing time for pubs in rural Ireland was a moveable feast. Drinking laws were flexible, and if rules were bent a little on occasion, there wasn't too much fuss made about it. I did get very tired from working late so often. In saying that I did enjoy the craic so much that often, I didn't want to go home! When I knew there was going to be a long night ahead, I would run home, change my clothes and come back for the night shift, so much so that on occasion, the customers jokily asked me, 'Have you no home to go to?' It was funny, because they themselves moaned and protested when last drinks were actually served.

It would have been strange if there hadn't been the odd ruckus, as there is in every pub at some stage. Even at moments like that, Sean would have it all under control. He would come in with a hose and would ask the peaceful punters to step aside. Then he would give those hot under the collar a nice gentle cold shower, saying, 'That'll cool you down now, boys!' On other occasions, if someone dared to answer the call of nature against the wall of the pub, Maura, Sean's wife, would throw a bucket of water over them. If they shouted at her, she'd say, 'Oops, sorry, I'm just watering the flowers.'

Many the laugh we had back then. Any troublemakers were barred on the night but the next night they would come back like meek sheep and apologise, imploring, 'Can we come back, please?' The prodigal children were let back in, under strict orders to behave. Sean looked after the punters and his staff as if they were family. He made sure everyone connected to the place was happy and safe and inspired great loyalty as a result.

Sometimes famous people came into the pub to sample our renowned warm and welcoming atmosphere. Of course, we always had our own local celebrities, a lot of whom were popular sportspeople. We had the GAA football and hurley brigade, Irish rugby and soccer stars, and even a few cricketers who became semi-regulars. As I said, I had married one of these cricket-mad lads so was never at a loss for words when it came to discussing their sport whenever they were around. I feel it would not be right for me to name any of them because they were entitled to their anonymity while they were enjoying their night out and a quiet pint. It didn't matter anyway—big star, local farmer or tradesman—they were all the same to me: customers in the pub.

When I was well settled into the job Sean allowed me to take charge of the bar when he was not around. He knew I was capable of looking after the place and would never let him down. I used to be quite happy to sort everything out at the bar and look after the staff by myself. I knew I was with people I could trust and admire, and I knew they trusted and respected me.

I have always been aware of energy in buildings, and the feeling of joy and happiness in the pub was really special. When the customers came in they left their stress at the door. It was a place where they could get some release and respite from the struggles of daily life.

Some of the regulars could be a bit bold on occasions. A couple of them liked to put ice down my back when I wasn't looking, and cracked up laughing as they watched me squirm. After this happened a few times, I got a bit fed up, so one evening I filled a pint glass full of water and threw it straight at the latest jokester who had just put ice down my back. Unfortunately, for me, at the last second he quickly moved out of the way and a lady sitting beside him at the bar got drenched. Oops! To make matters worse, she turned out to be a friend of the lead singer in the band that was playing that night.

Straight away, Sean came on the scene and told me to go outside and cool down, and he would have a chat with me when he got a break. Oh no, I thought, I'm in trouble now. Who would blame him? After all, showering his customers was not in my job description.

I went out to the beer garden, which was furnished with several tables and chairs. I sat down on the swing seat, a special feature included in this space, and nervously waited to be reprimanded. Talk about something backfiring! I knew I shouldn't have done what I did in the first place, but I was only having a bit of fun. And then, the more I thought about it, the more I thought how funny the situation was. Despite myself I got a fit of the giggles.

I sobered right up, though, when Sean came out. He sat down and told me to tell him exactly what happened. When I finished relaying my tale, to my surprise and relief he laughed and said the "drenched" woman wasn't that wet at all, and she had been looked after by the staff and didn't take umbrage about what happened to her. So, we all kissed and made up, and we were all happy families again, phew! Needless to say I got some stick after that for a bit.

You'd have some smart lads at the bar shouting, 'Duck!' when I came into the room or, 'Hey, Kathleen, did you come down in the last shower?' and even, 'Kathleen, could I have some water, but preferably in a glass?' What could I do but smile sweetly and take the slagging.

That was the way JD's was: a place of fun and frolics where you had to be able to give and take stick every now and then.

I will always remember Italia 1990, the year the Irish football team made it to the quarter-finals of the World Cup. What a journey the whole nation had. It really was a once-in-a-lifetime experience, and I have never seen the like of it since. Everyone in Ireland grew at least a foot taller with national pride and fervour. Our heroes were Ireland's coach, Jack Charlton, his assistant Maurice Setters and the Irish football team.

The Irish fans who went to support the team in Italy were also fantastic: win, lose or draw, they were there to celebrate and were great ambassadors for our country and our people. As Ireland progressed through to the knockout stages, we all excitedly watched the matches on the TV while wearing the green shirts of the Irish team. What a rollercoaster ride it was. The Irish colours were plastered everywhere you looked in Ireland and JD's was no different with flags and bunting inside and out. I don't know if we closed the pub at all during that time. We had a duty and responsibility to make sure the party had a home and the drinking and the singing and the laughter just kept going on and on.

There is a wealth of archive footage and photographs from that time, and if you look back, you can see what a fantastic lift was given to the whole country. Over a few weeks, we were all united as Jackie's Army. In the lead-up to the matches, a lot of customers enjoyed talking about the upcoming games. All the lads at the bar, even rugby lads, became football pundits overnight.

One time someone shouted out disparagingly that Charlton was English, and we shouldn't be supporting him, and another individual retorted, 'No, he is not. The great, great, grandmother of his dog was Irish and anyway, he is a Geordie, and we are claiming rights over him.' He must have been the most-loved Englishman ever to grace these shores. If he'd gone forward for election as Irish president, the people would unanimously have voted for him. Although we may not have won the World Cup, I guarantee you, internationally, we won it for how we celebrated.

Come on the lads! It is not often in Kerry that Gaelic games lose centre stage to soccer, but for that moment in Ireland's history, it did. It was absolutely unreal, and I was really lucky to be working there when Irish fervour was at its peak. The local Irish pub became a focal point for the Irish community right across Ireland and the whole experience was just fabulous.

Every now and again when times are quiet in my life, I sit and think back to my time in JD's. I don't regret a moment of all the years I spent there. I often think of the customers, several of whom I still count as dear friends. For some time after I stopped working there, on the odd occasion—when possible—I dropped over to the pub and enjoyed catching up with staff I knew back in the day who were still working there. They always welcomed me as part of their pub family, and I was truly honoured to count them as treasured friends and grateful for the fantastic memories we shared.

Unfortunately, as I write this story, JD's has passed into history, and it lives now only in my heart and in the hearts of those with whom I shared so many moments. Some have passed into spirit, and I have no doubt these fine people regaled the angels about how JD's brightened up their lives in that very special Irish pub. I am also sure that my great friend Sean is up there telling stories and making friends, getting laughs and sharing his love on the other side. Ar dheis De a Anam. May he rest in peace.

Chapter 9
The Hospital Lottery

I think back to the little family we were then: Tony, myself and James, the little miracle who brought great joy into our lives. I was also aware of Michael, our angel in heaven who was parked at my shoulder and whom I was sure would be there to help James throughout his life. They say it is good to count your blessings, and I do. I also believe we shouldn't hold onto our pain, because then we will never develop, never change. We need to keep on striving forward, and know that life is not always bad and at times can actually be beautiful and wonderful.

The next part of my hospital journey was to show, yet again, what a lottery life can be. I always wanted a large family, and it wasn't long before I got pregnant again, despite being warned of the risks. I knew there was a possibility I could lose the baby, but I had great faith. The success of the second pregnancy meant I had hope that I might be gifted with another baby, another success, but this time the pregnancy only lasted three months and three days.

That was when my little daughter Lizzie went home to heaven. I was distraught. I really had hoped and prayed, but this time it was not to be.

On the day I lost Lizzie, I was feeling pain, and so after the previous experiences, I went straight to hospital. When I was seen, I was sent immediately to the theatre and when I woke up later in the recovery room, my baby was gone. Again, there was no funeral, no burial site, no knowledge of where my little girl had gone. I kept trying to accept that I now had two angels in heaven, but I could not describe my unbearable grief. A line from a poem written by Patrick Pearse about lost children comes to mind: 'Lord, thou art hard on mothers: we suffer in their coming and their going.'

How true those words were. To lose babies is bad enough, but I never even got to hold Lizzie or Michael. The only way I knew they were real was because I had felt their tiny beings inside me. They had been real all right.

My little lost girl released a well of tears in me, and at one stage, I didn't think I was ever going to stop crying. I was just thirty years old, and I thought I had enough pain to last a lifetime. My heart goes out to women who have lost babies or find it hard to have children because I do understand from personal experience what they are going through.

Now, I can say I feel blessed to have had my two little angels. I believe they had their purpose, and that they have been with me since, throughout my life. I know that our spiritual connection is infinite. I now accept that the grief I have suffered showed me how much I wanted them, and how glad I was to be their mum. Coming to terms with their loss has somehow given them back to me, and I know I will be with them again at some stage in the future.

I have to say working in JD's pub helped. The atmosphere in the pub was always uplifting, but it did take quite some time to fully heal and recover my smile, so it could come from my heart again and wasn't the fake version that sat on my face to mask the pain.

After all I went through, it was not until 1996 that I got pregnant again. Some people asked me why I put myself through another pregnancy, and all I can say is I wanted a little brother or sister for James. I would have been happy with either but secretly I probably hoped for the set, a little boy and a little girl.

Of course, all the old fears and worries came flooding back again. I was disappointed that Dr Creedon, the kind doctor who looked after me during my previous pregnancies, had retired. The new obstetrician seemed satisfactory, even though it took me a while to relax and trust him. I put this down to my mental and emotional state.

Understandably, my anxieties and fears ran very high. I would cry very easily and was tetchy with everyone because I was so worried things might go wrong. Pregnancy for me was a nightmare, a really scary time. I desperately wanted this child, so I had to live with my pain and fears. But what I was to experience next was on a whole different level.

At that point, Tony and I had been living in a house in Ballybunion owned by my father-in-law, but the plan was always to build in Lahardane, a townland not far from Ballybunion. Tony had taken it upon himself to build our new home there, but before the house was even halfway constructed, the father-in-law put the house we were living in up for sale. It sold quickly, and we had to leave the premises and live in my sister-in-law's house for six months before we could move into our brand-new home.

I know that life is always full of ups and downs, but right then everything really did seem very difficult. It wasn't an ideal time to get pregnant, but what can you do? I was aware I had to take things as easy as I could. After the house was sold, I found myself packing up our home into a trailer as we prepared to move. My dad was a great help, and we had a fair few giggles together.

Dad could get a laugh out of a stone, and he always knew how to cheer me. Of course, my hubby still had to go to work and so did I because we needed the income to finish building our new house. As quickly as we could, we finished our packing and made the temporary move to my sister-in-law's house. That was interesting, two women in a kitchen, one pregnant and quite emotional at the time, and the other one used to doing things her own way. It was a rainy summer that year, and as our house was being built beside my sister-in-law's, the rain and muck made my in-law's house look like a building site as well. I will never forget that summer.

At times, my patience would get the better of me, because I longed for my new home to be finished. They say a watched kettle never boils and to look out of the window each day and see what I thought was a lack of progress was at times soul-destroying.

One day, the heavens opened, and down poured the rain. The house I was living in looked dreadful, and the whole place was sodden and mucky. Everything was a mess. As if that wasn't bad enough, if we lit the fire (and we often had to because it was miserable and cold), the house filled with smoke, which often resulted in me feeling nauseous as well as finding it hard to breathe. The fact that our clothes were covered in smoke a lot of the time drove me bananas.

My mum was so good to me, and she frequently came over to try and help me clean the house, which was an ongoing battle. She would also help us clean the range that we later discovered had a bit missing in it, which had caused the problem with the smoke. I swore I would never have one of those yokes in my new home—ever.

On the evening of 6th January, I felt unwell, and when I went to the toilet I saw my urine was brown. In terror, I rang the hospital, and they said that I was in labour. However, since I didn't have any labour pain I was concerned. Surely, if I was in labour, I should have *some* pain! I was really afraid. Tony called my mum, and she came scurrying over to our house.

She looked as scared as I felt. She said she would take care of little James, while Tony and myself went to the hospital. God bless her, I think my mum must have had very sore knees from bending God's, Mary's and all the other angels' and saints' ears so much so that her child and grandchild could go through the birth process safely.

I will never forget the weather we had that night. It was snowing, and we were very stressed. The car slipped and slid on the road as we made our way to the hospital. It was something like three minutes after midnight when we got to the place. When we arrived I had to walk into the ward.

There was no nice caring nurse waiting for me with a wheelchair like there was with my first pregnancy, no soothing words spoken. In truth, the staff were not best pleased to see me arriving at such a late hour of the evening. All I was told was that I would be fine, but I was beginning to feel very unwell. I slowly paced up and down the hospital corridor for what seemed an age before a man came along and said he had a bed for me.

After a while a hospital doctor examined me and told me yes, I was in labour. But I told the doctor there was something else going on, which I felt was different from labour pains, and my feeling of discomfort and sickness was getting worse. But no matter how much I insisted, he didn't listen to me.

The hours passed and morning came. I couldn't stay in the bed and relax as I was very unsettled, and was up and down to the loo very frequently. Then a nurse came over to me. I recognised her and felt slightly relieved. She checked me and said, 'You are two centimetres.' She left, and I lay back in the bed.

After a while, I felt myself becoming really drowsy. When the nurse came back a while later, I told her in a slurred voice that I was seeing a crowd of people and a beautiful angel flying over me. Then I said, 'I am flying toward my angel.'

I didn't realise my spirit had separated from my body until I looked back and saw myself in the bed. From this vantage point, I saw the nurse suddenly going into a panic and rushing to get the doctor. The paediatrician, Dr Leahy, came straight away. When he saw me, he said, 'We need to get this woman to theatre now. It doesn't look good. She might die, and we may also lose the baby. We need to operate straight away.'

Dr Leahy told the hospital gynaecologist of his fears. He concurred with Dr Leahy's recommendation and went to scrub up and get ready for an emergency C-section. I had no idea what was going on at the time. I had separated within myself, and although I could get a bird's eye view of the drama around me, I wasn't cognitive enough to know what was actually happening. Later, I was told more about the pandemonium of that evening and learned that the doctor said he would do his best to save both of us. It was touch and go.

The gynaecologist told Tony to call in all the family to say their goodbyes as there was a good chance that I might not survive the operation. Tony was in a daze and someone took him away for a bite to eat while the operation was being done, just to distract him a little bit during this awful time. But I knew my partner, and that his heart and spirit were with me in the theatre.

At that time, I was floating above everything, away in my own world. I can only imagine what Tony was going through, the poor man. He had already grieved the loss of Michael and Lizzy, and now he might lose this little baby *and* me. Much later, I pieced together some fragments of what happened from a few friends and family and staff members who were present at the time. The reports were unclear and incomplete, but subsequent events gave me the information I have now which made sense of the traumatic journey I endured.

Miraculously, both the baby and myself survived the operation but to help me recover I was put in an induced coma. My little girl was placed in a baby incubator unit and Dr Leahy looked after her like she was his own. He was an incredible guy, and no wonder he specialised in paediatrics. He was really hands on, even feeding and changing my baby, and over time, he became a close friend and hero to our family.

I believe it is thanks to him that my little Nora and I lived. We often speak about him and the heroic lengths he went to in order to save my baby and myself. This kind doctor will be forever in our hearts for the gift he gave us. I have to say he and Dr Creedon did their profession proud.

Dr Leahy consulted with his colleague, the gynaecologist who operated on me when he thought it was time for me to wake up. However, the nurse and some of the other doctors who looked after me were not sure it was a good idea to take me out of the coma at that moment in time. But Dr Leahy was insistent, and eventually, it was agreed I should be brought back very gently.

As I came to, I was pretty confused and disorientated, and convinced that my baby was lost. Even though Dr Leahy told me I had a beautiful baby girl, I didn't believe him. I hadn't any memory of giving birth, and only remembered the traumatic events before my surgery. It actually upset me that the doctor even named my child when he was talking about her. I know Tony and I had a name picked out for her, but my emotions were all over the place at that time. I am sure the doctor understood this.

'Nora Lisa fought very hard to stay here,' he said to me.

'You've made a mistake,' I told him. 'I'd know if I had a child.'

The truth is, now I know that some women during similar traumas have difficulty in accepting a child's birth because when they are heavily anaesthetised, they are often unaware of the actual birth taking place.

At that point in time, my daughter was still being looked after in the baby care unit, and on the doctor's suggestion, a nurse went and took a photo of her and showed me the picture. The little baby I looked at was really beautiful, but I still couldn't believe she was mine. Dr Leahy knew I needed to physically connect with my baby and the next thing I knew, little Nora was brought to me and put in my arms. Even as I held her I found it hard to believe she was mine.

I hadn't had a chance to build that connection, that bond a mother gets when a baby is placed in her arms straight away after it is born. Was this all a trick of the mind? Was I dreaming? Dr Leahy left Nora with me that night so the two of us could make up for lost time. It turned out to be exactly what I needed. As I realised Nora was really there with me, my own beautiful little baby girl, I cried tears of joy and relief.

It was Dr Leahy and the nurses and the angels who saved our lives. I am so grateful to him now, but I paid a huge price for what happened. In the aftermath of the birth, I looked like a wounded soldier back from the war. I was cut to ribbons, and the horrific tale my body would reveal in due course would show that something went badly wrong in the surgery. It left me believing that it was prayer and not the skill of the surgeon who saw me through this horror.

Even though he had the records detailing the birth of my son James, the surgeon ignored all the risks that had been documented by Dr Creedon. As I mentioned, when I first met him, he seemed fine, but I found it hard to trust him. Now I know he never managed my pregnancy in the right way. If he had, he could have saved me a lot of the medical problems I had later on.

Doctors nowadays are being held more and more accountable for their actions. Back then you just had to trust and get on with it. Medical negligence was not a thing and mistakes were generally buried.

Dr Creedon's care that brought James's birth to a happy conclusion was totally ignored and that man nearly lost me and my fourth baby. If it was not for the incredible skill and care of Dr Leahy and the nursing team, I am sure neither Nora nor I would be here.

In the records, it was written that I would have real problems in holding onto a baby full-term. It was so well-documented by Dr Creedon that I believe that if the gynaecologist had followed his lead, things would have been so much better. What he did almost caused me to lose not only my life but also that of my princess, Nora. The problems this event caused have continued to affect me and my daughter up to the present day. Also, the bond that was interfered with between mother and child, along with the length of time I spent in the hospital trying to recover did tremendous emotional damage to both of us.

It took five long years of tears, stress and night terrors for me and my little baby girl before we eventually settled down and things began to improve. I have to say Tony did a great job when little Nora was born and kept in close contact with her all the time she was in the incubator. If he hadn't, then I feel the bond between the baby and ourselves would have been even harder to develop. Nora and I have come a long way, but the trauma and feelings of loss and grief will always be there. You physically, mentally and emotionally never forget something like that.

After finally being released home with my daughter, it wasn't long before I was rushed back to the hospital, bleeding heavily and, as you can imagine, very distraught. The same gynaecologist made an attempt to stop my bleeding and then sent me home again. However, that did not solve the problem and the bleeding persisted. Finally, I called my GP, and he sent me to the Bon Secours in Cork as an emergency, and I was put under the care of a wonderful woman doctor called Rachel. After carefully examining me, I was rushed into surgery, and she performed a partial hysterectomy on me.

Of course, I had no knowledge of what was going on, and it was only after the operation that the doctor told me what she had to do. She had no choice, and it was the only course of action she could take in order to save my life. Although this awful news almost broke my heart, because I knew there was no chance of me having another child, I had no option but to come to peace with this reality.

There was no doubt that Rachel had saved my life. What followed was a long stay in the hospital. It so happened that the doctor went on holiday just after my operation, but she left strict instructions that I was not to go home until I was completely recovered. Mum and Tony looked after James and Nora, and this meant I was on my own quite a lot in the hospital, which was a good distance from my home in Ballybunion.

I felt lonely, and the experience was reminiscent of the time I felt abandoned in the hospital in Tralee as a child. I don't know how we all survived during this awful time, but then Tony was a good man, my Mum was wonderful, and we did our best and muddled through somehow. Someone once said what does not kill you makes you stronger. I'm not so sure of that, but I did survive.

The days seemed to be so long, and eventually, I got fed up. I felt I was there so long I was practically one of the staff members! But the doctor was right, I needed space to heal. When she returned from holidays, the doctor gave me a thorough check-up and told me I could go home and reconnect with my family.

So finally I was let out. However, after a very short time at home, I developed pains in my lower abdomen. I thought, Oh no, not again. I had an ultrasound done and was told I had a cyst on my ovaries, which had not been removed during the partial hysterectomy. It never rains, but it pours. So back into hospital again. I tell you, I should have a ward called after me.

Up to then, whenever I was in hospital I was in a private room, but this time I was put in a six-bed ward, and had people to talk to. It broke the day up and controlled my natural impatience to escape. The girls in the ward and I had great craic together. I was such a regular that the matron, who had got to know me, offered me a private room when one became available. I turned it down because I was far happier being in the ward with people. All in all, it did me the world of good that I stayed where I was.

On the morning, I was going for the surgery, the doctor talked about taking my ovaries out during the operation. This doctor was one I hadn't met before. I said, 'Hold on, I had been previously told that the operation was just to remove the cyst from one of my ovaries.'

'Oh, is that right?' the doctor said. 'I will check the documentation.'

He did, and when he came back he said it was recommended for my ovaries to be removed along with the cyst. 'But when we go in for the operation we will see what we need to do to avoid more problems in the future.'

'Fair enough,' I agreed. By that stage, I had surrendered. 'Do what is necessary.'

He was a nice doctor, and I had a feeling he would take good care of me. When I woke up the doctor came over to me. He was not a happy bunny. 'Catherine,' he said, 'You have no cyst. You never had one, and so I left the ovaries there and just closed you up.'

I knew straight away it was yet another blunder in a series of blunders. I could see he was angry that I had been put through an unnecessary surgery. I was beginning to get used to this. It was Sod's Law—anything that can go wrong will—and it did for me.

The most irritating part of the whole affair was that truth and clarity seemed to missing as by the time I had finished this journey of medical turmoil, I didn't feel there was any part of my femininity that had avoided the surgeon's knife on multiple occasions. I had no idea of the overall damage that was done to me or how long this saga would continue.

I had met some incredible doctors and medical staff during that period and had felt I had cheated death on too many occasions. If I was a cat, I would be running out of my nine lives pretty fast. All along, I could have done with one thing: the truth, and for every good doctor I met, I also seemed to encounter many who were in the wrong job. From where I was at this point in my life, it had made me very wary and afraid of hospitals and medical procedures.

After a while, believe it or not, I did develop a cyst in my tummy, and it grew to the size of a football. I looked like a beached whale. I was so big I felt that if you stuck a pin in me I'd go pop. I understand cysts are quite a common occurrence but still. Of course, this meant I had to go to the hospital to have it removed.

I was up to high doh and the stress was unbelievable. I prayed to my angels and saints for strength and kept my fingers crossed, and if I could have acquired a rabbit's foot and a four-leafed clover, I would have carried them into the operation room with me. I was so relieved when it was all over and thankfully the procedure went smoothly.

I have had to go to the hospital a number of times since then, and every time I do I feel a sense of fear and trepidation.

However, I am aware that without hospitals I would probably be dead.

Only last year, when I was getting a small operation done, my blood pressure went through the roof and only to the good care of the nurses and doctors, who knows what may have happened.

People like the doctor who hit me and the gynaecologist who was negligently left messes for other doctors to sort out. Thank God the good ones were there, otherwise my story could have been a lot worse. I might have had four little angels in heaven instead of two—and I may have been up there with them myself.

The scandals that have rocked the health system in recent years have made doctors more accountable, but I still find it unbelievable that in those days, in the 1980s and 1990s, some hospitals were less than thorough when employing people who may not have stood up to scrutiny or were not trained to the highest standards. Today things have greatly improved, and here in Ireland, we have several excellent medical schools with worldwide reputations. It is also well known that Irish nurses and doctors are sought after across the globe.

Nonetheless, those who appoint doctors as GPs and surgeons in hospitals should be ever-cautious and vigilant in ensuring that the medical personnel employed are indeed fit for purpose and have the training and standards for the jobs they are hired for. Those who employ them have an important responsibility because the lives of the patients they treat are at stake.

I will be forever grateful for the care and attention of those very special doctors and nurses who helped me through extremely challenging times and ensured that James and Nora survived. And not only did they survive, they have both now grown up and are living their own lives. My son is in a great relationship and has healthy and beautiful children of his own, and my daughter is a very gifted artist. I have indeed been blessed.

Chapter 10
The Road to Recovery

Because of all the traumatic events which happened to me in the hospital, it was a long time before I was able to deal with the damage that had been done to me both physically and mentally. On top of that, my emotions were all over the place. Furthermore, as a result of the induced coma I was put into after Nora's birth, I was robbed of the incredible experience of giving birth to my child and holding her in my arms. For James, I got to hold my little bundle of joy. With Nora, I didn't.

It taught me what a privilege it was to have your new baby close to your breast and feel the gentlest touch or breath on your skin. In those early days, it is also so important to hear the sounds and watch the movements the infant makes as it gets used to a brand-new world. It is also wonderful to see the little smiles you are sure are for you, even though others might say it was just wind. These special moments and much more were lost forever.

All this meant I didn't have the connection I should have had with the baby. In fact, for the first year after Nora was born, I actually grieved her loss even when she was with me. She was a sickly child and suffered from seizures and convulsions. She was also prone to stress, which included crying a lot and not sleeping well, and it took her about five years before she settled into a calmer and more normal routine. She was really precious to me, but those early years were heartbreaking.

To see my little infant in such distress constantly and feel incapable of making it right for her was frustrating and difficult. I felt utterly helpless at times and useless as a mother. Of course, there were lovely moments of joy, but pain and worry were my constant companions in the early years.

I also found it hard to rest. After Nora's birth, I was in severe depression and ill for almost a year and a half. I had changed through all that had gone on. My body was in tatters, and I felt abandoned and unheard by everyone. The traumatic events in the hospital had left me physically scarred and mutilated and though the damage did subside, the marks of the surgeon's knife would always be there to be seen.

I know I was probably hard to live with then as I was often morose and angry, and I was definitely not the life and the soul of the party. I will be forever grateful to my mum who helped me a lot, minding my babies and trying to take care of me. I found it difficult to come out from a wall of protection I had created around me. I felt the world was not safe anymore and would never be safe again. This surly prison I had put myself into was my own personal hell. I was a victim and felt I had little or no control over what happened to me.

I went through the motions of living but all I had left was deep despair and pain. At that time, I wasn't much involved in beautifying our new home as I just wasn't up to it. I was lost in a dark, never-ending tunnel. Tony did his best to keep the ship afloat and, with my mum's help, they plastered over the cracks and kept things going as best they could. The new house was a dormer bungalow and Tony built a beautiful bathroom with a big comer bath for me which was very fancy for its time.

In the mood I was in, it was just as well that we already had furniture from our previous house because I had no motivation at all to decorate the place. Creating a home was far from my mind at the time. Death would have been a more preferable option in those dark days. I did, at one stage, plant red and white roses in the garden, but in general it really depended on how I felt on a particular day. Everything was about one day at a time, and there were more bad days than good.

I gave up my job at JD's because I had to concentrate on survival and trying to look after my babies. It was the end of an era in the pub, but at least I could look back on that job with the fondest of memories. I felt so sorry for Nora because she was sick a lot, and she couldn't understand why. We could do little more than be there for her and nurse her through her pain.

On too many occasions, she had difficulty breathing after a convulsion, which was terrifying, and we had to dash to the doctor to save her life.

Over the following number of years, things slowly improved. Her breathing normalised, and her convulsions stopped. There were many ups and downs, but we did have some really happy moments. Tony constructed a large shed at the back of the house which gave him plenty of room to work on his carpentry career, which created more hope for a better tomorrow.

James started school and loved it, something he certainly didn't take from me! He was a very sociable child with a magnetic warmth. However, Nora, whose physical health was thankfully getting better, wasn't too fond of the idea of playschool. It was she who reminded me of myself as a child. In time, though she calmed down and gradually adapted to school life.

Then in 2007, at the age of seventy-six, my lovely dad passed away, a man who had been my rock and an ever-constant in my life. I was heartbroken. My hero had left, and my grief was intense. No more would I hear his music and laughter, which had always lightened my life. He was a gentle soul and the two of us had shared many a laugh over the years.

Before he passed, I would help him sneak out to buy cigarettes. I would take him away from under the watchful gaze of a well-meaning wife (my mum) and some of my other siblings, so he could have a few puffs of forbidden pleasures. Of course, he should have given up the ciggies, as they were bad for him, but as time wore on the damage was done, and I felt it wouldn't have made any difference anyway. I suspect all the family knew what he was up to, but for me, I felt he was finding spare time with me, so we could talk, and the ciggies were really just an excuse.

It is only now I really understand he was trying to help me heal, in his quiet way. I remembered back to my childhood when my donkey died, how he comforted me by taking me on walks and taking moments out of his day to spend time with his lost little girl. He knew me so well and had so much wisdom.

When she was small, Nora wanted her dad and I to mind her all the time, and she would go into hysterics if she thought we were going out anywhere. She was so afraid of being left alone and abandoned, and it was all very stressful. Dad's death, then, on top of all that stress was very hard to take.

I needed something to take my mind off the turmoil, and it came by way of the carpentry business that Tony took over. He had worked in the trade with his two uncles since he was a young lad of seventeen. Now, twenty-five years later, one of the uncles died and the other uncle had a heart attack. The opportunity came up to take over the business but the decision had to be made quickly. Tony is a hard worker, and between the two of us, we thought we had what it took to make the business work, and I really believe, to this day, that with the proper support, we would have built a really good company together. But life doesn't always work out as planned.

For my part, the sadness around the loss of the babies and the depression that came after all that happened in the hospital meant that there were times my mind was elsewhere when I should have been concentrating on the business. I have no doubt that the medication I was given also had a part to play in making it difficult to achieve what I wanted to do. I found it almost impossible to trust people, and for whatever reason or whatever lessons we had to learn, we both unknowingly attracted untrustworthy people into our lives. Over the following couple of years, we were cheated on and stolen from on a number of occasions.

It was a very tough time for Tony, myself and my little family. The accountants, the banks and others who handled our money helped themselves to some of our finances, but we did open the door to that by trusting the wrong people too much. We really were quite inexperienced in the ways of business and perhaps too naive. We also weren't aware of the horror stories relating to banking and other financial institutions that were happening at the time.

I don't think either of us could have worked harder, and the lack of financial success added to our emotional strain. However, along the way, we met some fantastic people whom I still remember fondly today. These individuals really helped and supported us as we tried to make our business work. I do believe that those who abused our trust and told lies will have to answer for what they have done at some stage. I have seen karma turn around already for some of them and bite them on the backside. No doubt some of them thought they could destroy us, but they didn't succeed.

Tony and I are as strong as we always were and getting stronger. My love and admiration for him will never die. If we were not as strong as we are I have no doubt we would have been destroyed and our family would have fallen apart.

Tony has skilled hands, and he is a gifted craftsman. To this day, I pass by some of the work we did together and look at these jobs with pride. I have no doubt that our work will stand the test of time. Even though the business didn't go as well as we'd hoped, we can take away many positive things from our venture.

We made fantastic business connections throughout the country, and I learned so much in the process, from accounting to web design, to producing top-quality brochures. I found out I could do an awful lot more than I thought I could. The connections I made taught me how to persevere and not give up.

After the business folded, we had to endure. It took a while for us to recover and move on, but we eventually did. Tony started working again as a freelance carpenter, and I found work in another pub, so we were on the up again. Today he is still a carpenter and makes a living at what he loves, using his hands to create things.

No more do we have the overheads or headaches of the past, and instead we have contentment in our work. We have survived and life has got better. I started to find my smile again and promised myself to take the good out of these life lessons and challenges and move on. I know how much courage we have, Tony and I, and we trust that God is always looking out for us.

As I look back over the years, I realise that darkness prevented me from shining my light for a long time. But, eventually, I started to really fight back, and I learned to see myself as a bright and gifted person. It was life and not the education system that helped me see that. All the school gave me was criticism from teachers and lots of negative labels. At that time in Ireland, you did not rise above your station, and if you did, you were frowned upon. People would say things like, 'Who does she think she is, getting notions about herself?'

I know now I was dyslexic, not stupid, but for a time, I believed I was. I believed I was not good enough and not bright enough. Now I know I just learn differently than the way I was being taught. The school system itself has evolved since then. It is clear that the methodology of teaching in those days was not sufficient to get the best out of the children in their care.

If I am shown something in a clear and patient way, I learn really fast. For sure, teachers back in the day were only doing what they were trained to do. Now I am sure they would see the error of their ways.

I wouldn't say that today we know everything about education and the best way to support and develop our children, but things have improved. This is because we are learning more and more as the years go by. It was only recently I read about the great Austrian philosopher and social reformer, Rudolf Steiner. He really was ahead of his time. Back in the early 1900s, he proposed a holistic style of education.

He recognised the need for children to become free and autonomous human beings in a secure environment of warmth and care, in which the individuality of the child can find its own potential. But until recently society ignored his wise words, and teachers continued to teach in a strict, authoritarian way, which gave no space for individuals to develop and find their unique creativity inside themselves.

Children do not perform well when they are afraid, and when they don't understand what is going on they switch off and detach. This severely affects their ability to learn, leaving these children even more frightened and insecure, and judged as inferior.

With the support of the child paramount, teachers are now slowly moving towards truly child-centred education, creating an atmosphere where children can shine and manifest their gifts and talents. I'm sure the future will be brighter because of it, and I believe it really is a step in the right direction. It seems to be the way of life that new and innovative ideas take a long time to be accepted by society, but it also looks like the speed of change is quickening to match the needs of our evolving world.

It is interesting to note that this once "stupid little child" is writing her story now and has been chosen by divine will to help people on their life paths. Obviously, God knows what He created in me and is now helping me to shine my light—but I often wonder why He had to do it the hard way!

The level of abuse I suffered as a child and through my teenage years almost took away my soul. I hated to be seen as an attractive woman as it just did not feel safe to be wanted or desired. For a long time, I was unable to celebrate the woman I was back then. Now, due to my evolving self-esteem, and with Tony by my side, I am now proud to be a woman and to carry my feminine energy within. I am able to be loved, to show love, to be intimate and open and to be sensual and free.

Despite mutilation scars and hurts I am still, and will always be, the beautiful woman whom God created, and no abuser is going to take that away from me anymore. The tomorrows I live will not be dictated by the evils of yesterday.

Chapter 11
A Celestial Tale

Some say we choose the type of life we will live before we come to Earth. If that is so, I might justifiably not choose to work for Spirit as it is definitely not the easiest journey. A song sung by Meatloaf says, 'Life is a lemon, and I want my money back.' This could be understandable in the context of my life. I spent the first half of my life in suffering, if you like, clearing some of the karmic issues I came in with and gaining an understanding of suffering. Then, in the second half of my life I was able to translate that pain into growth, so I could serve the common good and help other travellers find their way out of pain and tears.

In pondering these thoughts, I considered that if I agreed to these things, maybe my spirit needed its head examined! I found myself talking to God and said to Him, 'It might be an idea if we had a blueprint to follow, God! The North Star you gave us is faith, but then it's just like Christopher Columbus, you're on your own with no map.'

I know we have free will, but I would like to believe God and the angels are there to help when needed. All I really know at the end of the day is that we are on a journey and that at times, it feels like someone is out to get us. At least that is what it felt like for me. I believe many others have experienced life like that too.

I often imagine how we were chosen for our particular journeys while in heaven. Maybe a certain number of us are lined up and God says, 'Listen, lads, we need some volunteers to go to Earth to be healers and psychics and therapists and mediums.'

I am a bit distracted and don't notice most of the others stepping back and leaving a small group of us "volunteers" standing on our own.

'Next time, I'll pay more attention. I won't be caught again like this,' I grumble.

I hear a few others muttering along the line, going something like, 'Ah not again.'

But a grateful, loving God says: 'I knew I could depend on you guys to volunteer to help the world. You have taken the spiritual path, and it will be through your hard work and sacrifice that the world can change. I'm sure you'll be delighted to know that crucifixion is not done on earth nowadays and the burning at the stake is also generally out as well. Good positive strides forward for mankind. I know some of you have been to Earth many times before, and have bravely taken a spiritual path a few times in the past. You have my admiration, respect, and all my love.

'We will have a special party for you this evening before you head on your way and incarnate. In celebration of your courage, we will have a very special performance by the angelic choir who have been practising really hard for tonight's occasion. All of us up here want to give you a send-off that you will remember, one that will go deep into your subconscious and give you a constant inner knowing that there is light at the end of the tunnel.

'Regardless of how challenging it is down there, you will eventually make it home. You will be delighted to know that we have banned some of the entertainment songs that they had at the last farewell party. We sort of felt they were inappropriate based on the journey you were going on. We did not think "The Ring of Fire" was really appropriate and "Cool Clear Water" lost its attraction for those of you who experienced drowning as a witch in the Middle Ages.

'There will be the usual angel therapy before you go to Earth. As we know, it helps reconcile you with your choices. It is advised that when you get your mission, talk to your angel therapist so that between both of you, you can set aside support that may be accessed at certain times in your incarnation. It will help make things a little easier and help you know you aren't on your own. You'll know that we are always there, supporting you every step of the way. My gracious thanks as always, you are all fantastic, and I wish you a bon voyage.'

In those heavenly realms, as I think about my future journey, it annoys me to hear a group of chuckling spirits who dodged the bullet, hiding in the corner. But then the supervisor angels tell them not to laugh at the volunteers, saying, 'You know how it is—what goes around comes around.' That quietens them down. After a while, we are all friends again, and they join in and help the volunteers prepare for our forthcoming life on Earth. None of us at that time took the journey too seriously, as we know it is all part of a journey of learning and growth.

We even have the odd laugh about what we have agreed to on our adventure, but we try not to diminish it because some of us have taken a really tough road.

We collect our separate missions and negotiate the way the journey will unfold. I can imagine how my case goes:

'Well, dear one,' says the mission angel coordinator, 'We picked Ballybunion for you. It's in Kerry, in Ireland. We know you like the scenery and the place is quite beautiful. The weather is sort of temperate, neither too warm nor too cold. And you know the way you like playing in the puddles? Well, the Father thought the frequent rain of soft Irish days would suit you well.

'He thought His little girl would have so much fun in her wellies, and He said sometimes he may even come and join you down there and introduce you to other spiritual dimensions in the physical world. Kerry is particularly full of fairies and leprechauns.

'Ireland was once called the Land of Saints and Scholars so what a wonderful and historically rich place it will be to live in. A wise choice indeed. You will be going to the land of Saint Bridget, Saint Gobnait, Saint Colmcille and Saint Patrick, and you will be walking in their footprints. There will be a little bit of pain, the odd bit of abuse here and there, a small occasion of poisoning and possibly some difficulty with a few hospitals. In those institutions, you will shine a light which will show the great need to improve the administration problems there and help so many other people in the process. People like you help change the world. You should be proud of yourself and the contribution you will be making.

'You will have your own donkey and you, and he will be great friends, and a saint will come to visit you at times, along with the fairies. You'll have great contact with the spiritual world. The music and craic will be mighty, and it will be so good it will have you dancing in the street at times. Eventually, you'll do fantastic work in helping people. It will be wonderful, so just sign here and good luck.'

Seeing the coordinator angel's radiant and gentle smile, what else could I do? Of course, I was going to sign. After all, I knew the angels wouldn't steer me wrong.

I scribble my name on the contract. As I look back up, I see my angel therapist standing nearby, and she looks as if she needs a therapist herself, poor thing.

'Don't worry,' I say to her. 'How bad can it be?'

After a while, I hear a call from the dispatch department for me to be sent to Earth. By this stage, I have been given my personality and gifts for the trip as well as liaised with other spirits who would have an impact on my life to come. So there I am, seemingly aware of what I am doing and where I am going, but in truth oblivious to what really would lie ahead.

'Grand God, I'm ready to serve, let's go,' I say.

My spirit flies down to earth, and on a cool Irish morning in October, I arrive on this strange and beautiful planet. I am to be called Catherine and am happy to start my new adventure with my new identity.

While in this world we don't remember what our life before birth in heaven was like, not until we pass back into spirit. I'd like to think that we are one big, loving, kind and constantly evolving celestial family, always ready to assist each other on our journeys whenever truly needed.

My ever-changing life was to soon change again, and events were about to take place that would open me up to the next part of my journey. I would begin to live a life of service, along with experiencing a lot of profound healing, self-reflection and spiritual development. There was no doubt my angel therapist on the other side had her work cut out for her during the turbulent and transformational times that lay ahead.

Chapter 12
My Road to Damascus

I did enjoy the times I went to Mass but could hardly call myself devout. I suppose looking back on my history, I could see I was not happy with God because I felt He could have protected me better, and at times, he felt very distant from my life. That being said, I frequently called out to heaven for support when I felt abandoned, isolated and alone, which was all too often.

I think a lot of people do that—they cry out to God when they are in trouble and need help, but that doesn't mean they really believe He can help them. When something goes wrong, people say, God, why me? And if things then turn around for the better, more often than not, they say, I got a lucky break there, instead of thanking God for His help.

If it wasn't for my little family, I doubt I would be here today. I had no choice but to stay here and fight. Many times I found myself just going through the motions of living, just trying to survive. However, every now and again, despite myself, my natural compassion would creep out, and I would show care for another human being. When I became aware of what I was doing I would try to bury it or dismiss it as soon as I could in case it would make me seem vulnerable again.

One of the great joys I had in my life was watching my beautiful children play together, and then over time seeing them grow into independent adults. Their hope and laughter saw me through many a dark day, and I needed to be strong for them. Children are amazing. On a day you need a lift, they just say something or do something that can seem small but which can suddenly brighten up your world. It reminds you of how privileged you are to have them and how important it is for you to be there for them.

I was around forty-five years of age when Tony and I set about picking up the pieces after the demise of our business and started to try and move forward again. I didn't know it, but I was about to have a big reawakening to the world of Spirit, and I have no doubt that my dad, now in heaven, was part of the spirit team looking after me.

They say that when one door closes another door opens. In hindsight, I can see that I needed to let go of the past. Like so many other people, I could have been stuck with a sense of failure about certain events, but now I see the past as a stepping stone to my true purpose in life.

The events that would shape the next part of my life started when the priests of the parish planned a series of Padre Pio healing masses in the church in the village of Lixnaw, which was close to where I lived. It was part of a witness and healing ministry and followed in the tradition of St Pio of Pietrelcina who gave his life over to God's service. This holy man was born in the late nineteenth century. He became a priest and served in the parish of San Giovanni Rotondo on the east coast of Italy. Blessed with spiritual gifts which included the ability to heal, bilocation and prophecy, he also bore the stigmata of the wounds of Christ on his hands and feet.

The stigmata were a reminder that Jesus walked this earth and were a physical manifestation of the pain He carried. Padre Pio's story is one of immense faith and his dedication to the service of the sick is known globally. He was a real inspiration to me after helping to save my life from my drowning accident many years before.

A local lady who lived nearby had a very sad tragedy in her family and wanted to go to the Padre Pio Mass because she thought it might help her get through her grief. She asked me to drive her to the church because she didn't have a car. Eventually, I agreed to take her, but I was hardly enthusiastic about going. You'd think after my rescue by Padre Pio all those years ago I would have been delighted to go, but I felt a fearful kind of tug of war inside me. On the one hand, my heart and my spirit knew I needed to be there, but on the other hand, I resisted because God wasn't my best buddy at the time. He didn't really light my candle, so to speak.

At the time, I knew what it felt like to be a victim as God didn't rescue me from the medical profession even though I prayed for Him to help me. Sure, I still had my life and my two babies, but I felt that if God had really been on my team, I would have four healthy children and would have been fit and well and content in my own life.

Anyway, after a bit of gentle persuasion, reluctant as I was, we set off to the Mass. The lady who'd asked me to give her a lift had won the day. As far as I was concerned, I was only going to the Mass for her. Anyway, we arrived at the church which wasn't full when we got there. I was not really interested in the proceedings.

In fact, I was waiting for the whole thing to be over which of course didn't really make sense since I was, at least in my heart, devoted to the saint. But I was really detached from a lot of things at that particular moment in time and emotionally I was closed down for my own self-preservation.

I looked around and felt my anger rise when I saw what I deemed as some "shiny happy people" murmuring to each other. The lady with me noticed I was not in great humour and gave me a nudge.

'Come on, Catherine, try and focus a little bit,' she whispered. 'It's not all doom and gloom.'

I shifted in my seat and tried to settle myself. As I did, I suddenly became aware of a lot of giggling going on right behind me. I looked around, but there was no one there. Weird, I thought. Where were these sounds coming from? The church was small enough for me to see all the seats in it and as I peered about, all I saw were empty pews except for the small group of people I had seen further away, who definitely weren't giggling.

Then someone started to gently pull at my hair. What on earth was up? I glanced around, but no one was near me except my friend, who was sitting with her hands clasped. I was getting a bit freaked out. It couldn't be Spirit—could it? If it wasn't Spirit, was I losing my mind?

I stopped for a moment to consider the craziness of this and found myself thinking, 'OK, if this is Spirit or angels, you've got my attention. But please stop pulling my hair!' As I sat there wondering, I noticed that the mysterious giggles were actually lightening my mood, which was nice. It was amazing how infectious laughter could be.

This was all happening before the Mass started. In Ireland, starting times for events are quite flexible and the priests at Mass usually give people an extra bit of settling-in time. On that evening, this relaxed approach gave space for everyone to get their prayer books out and make themselves ready for this special time of healing and prayer.

By the time, the priest came out on the altar the church was full. He began the Mass by saying the Rosary. It had been a long time since I spoke these devotional prayers, and my recall was rusty regarding the specific words. Anyhow, I muddled through as best I could, mumbling and muttering as I went. When the Rosary was finished, a man, the first witness, went up to the altar to speak.

Apparently, he was to tell us an interesting story of how Padre Pio had positively affected his life. The congregation listened intently as the man talked about how Padre Pio had supported him and his family through pain, tragedy and loss. Completely unexpectedly, the story knocked me for six. Now, I was paying close attention, and I started to feel different about being there. All of a sudden, the hurt and anger I was carrying inside started to shift, and that gave space for light to shine through. My mood softened some more, and there was no question that I could definitely sense Spirit in the place.

Then, just before Communion, I looked at the altar and saw it suddenly light up with the most beautiful glowing light. Wow, I thought, that's amazing. But when I mentioned it to my friend beside me, she said she saw nothing. Was it all in my mind? First the giggling, then the hair pulling and now a bright light on the altar.

So I spoke to her again and asked her if she had heard anyone giggling earlier before the Mass started. She looked at

me curiously and said no, there was no giggling. I decided to say no more and the Mass ended without further incident.

On the way home afterwards, I couldn't stop thinking about what I'd experienced. Was I going mad? My mum always said I had a great imagination. I was suddenly brought back to when I was a child, sitting under the bridge at home, and I remembered I saw things other people did not see. In my heart, I knew that what I saw and felt in the church *was* real—I had not imagined it.

That night in bed I woke up to see a big red light glowing at the end of the bed. I could also feel someone pulling at my legs as if they were trying to get my attention. I felt a bit fearful and woke Tony up.

'Do you see a red light in the room, or feel anything strange?' I asked.

'No,' he replied. 'But you know the way sometimes you talk in your sleep and move around a bit? Well, tonight you fell asleep before I did, and I have to say you moved around an awful lot, even by your standards! It was so bad I was nearly pushed out of the bed! So come on, Catherine, calm down and go to sleep.'

I eventually did go back to sleep, but I continued to see the light for several nights afterwards. On those occasions, I didn't wake up Tony. There was no point, as I wasn't afraid any more. Now and again the light would be so bright it would light up the whole room. Sometimes it was a small blue light, sometimes a red one. Red in the church is often associated with Christ and blue is often linked to the Virgin Mary.

Then one night the room filled with spirits, the energetic remains of people from all walks of life. Again I was anxious, but really more intrigued than anything else. Why would

spirits be visiting me? Kerry people can be very friendly, so maybe they just dropped in for a cuppa. I giggled to myself with a sense of nervous awe at what was happening. Why should a little thing like being dead stop them? 'Sure you're as welcome as the flowers in May,' I found myself saying to them.

It had been a long time since I had seen spirits and beings from the elemental kingdom, and now I got the feeling I was starting to spiritually reawaken. This helped me remember the wonders I saw and experienced as a child. I wasn't sure what to do about it, and then I thought it might be an idea to light a few candles and pray for any of those spirits who needed a prayer. It took time to get into the practice of it, but eventually, I did, and as a result, I felt more peaceful in myself. I intuitively felt I was doing something right.

A few months later, another Padre Pio Mass was held, and this time I was eager to attend. At the end of the ceremony after Communion, I went up to get a blessing from a priest who had a little Padre Pio relic with him. When I received the blessing I collapsed. It was like my spirit detached from my body. I learned afterwards that the priest put me sitting on the chair and told everyone not to go near me, not to touch me, just to give me space. He explained that I'd have to come back slowly, only when my spirit was ready and when the angels would let me come back.

'Don't worry,' he said, 'She will be alright. I have seen this all before, so nobody needs to panic. All is in God's good hands.'

He told the lady who looked after the church to give me some water to drink when I came around. I regained consciousness after a few minutes and even though I thought

I was back to normal after a few sips of water I was still a bit wobbly and unsure underfoot when I left the church. I never thought of asking what had happened at the time and the priest never talked to me about it. I guess he was used to seeing unusual things like this happening at spiritual events. For him, it was just business as usual.

Apparently, it's something that Spirit does. During the charismatic movement, it happened regularly. It is known as "falling in the spirit". I believe that at some of these events, people used to also speak in tongues, and even though they didn't know the language they were speaking, others near them would often understand what they were saying. Strange things indeed.

By now, the Padre Pio Masses had become well-established in the community and the church was always packed. They ran from September to June, taking a break for the summer. On one particular month, the event was assisted by a second priest. We waited till near the end of the evening and then when the time came for the blessing with a Padre Pio relic my friend said she was content to stay in her seat, but asked me if I would get her rosary beads blessed.

'No problem,' I told her.

I went up to the altar and waited my turn. When the priest came towards me with the relic, without warning I collapsed to the ground. This was the second time I fell in the spirit. Two people came over, picked me up and put me sitting on a seat. Then they sat down on either side of me, so they could mind me.

Though I was out of it, I could hear everything that was going on. The priest, who was different from the priest who had experienced my first falling in spirit, came over to me and said, 'Wake up, woman, wake up.' I think he thought I was dead! As far as I was aware, I kept saying I wasn't, but no one seemed to hear me. Then he put his hands on either side of my face, covering my ears. I heard my ears go pop and all of a sudden I was back. The priest gently said, 'Take a few sips of water and then you'll be fine to go.'

At this point, my friend had come up to me and said I was as white as snow. I reassured her I was OK and that I'd just had another falling in spirit. By now, I was no longer afraid of these experiences.

This phenomenon of falling in spirit was something I experienced at a few more Padre Pio services, and I sort of got used to it. On another occasion, I was at a Padre Pio Mass with a few friends of mine, two of whom were sisters—cousins of Tony's—along with another girl who was a friend of the two sisters. One of the women went up to get rosary beads blessed for her grandson who was having heart surgery. While she was heading up to the altar, I went to get some holy water at the back of the church, after which I joined my friend at the altar for the blessing of the beads. At this part of the ceremony, I was holding the holy water in a burnt-out silver tealight holder.

The atmosphere was beautifully calm and peaceful, and only my friend and I were at the altar at that particular time. The priest blessed my friend's beads with Padre Pio's glove, and then he turned to me, whereupon I fell in spirit. I was put sitting in a seat and then the priest placed his hands over my ears. When he did this I regained consciousness. To everyone's surprise, the holy water I was holding did not spill.

After a while, I felt strong enough to get up and walk back to the bench I was originally sitting on with my friends. Upon returning to my seat I saw the look of surprise on one of my friend's faces. She whispered, 'You know, Catherine, when you were up at the altar and then turned around I could see right through your hands!'

I looked down to check my hands, but they just looked normal to me.

My friend was a little annoyed with me like I had somehow done this on purpose to her. She said, 'If I was not looking, I would never have believed it. I saw what I saw.'

I just shrugged and said, 'I can't explain it.'

She also said that she saw two holes in the bottom of the tealight holder I was carrying, but I said there couldn't have been. The holy water from the night light would have leaked out if there were. But my friend was vexed with me, and when the Mass was over she took the tealight holder and emptied out the water to show me the two holes—and there they were. I was as confused as she was and didn't have any answer for her.

After we left the church, there was only one thing that would calm us all down and restore our spirits, and that was, in time-honoured Irish tradition, to head to the pub for a drink and a chat about the evening's events.

Chapter 13
Witness

When we entered the pub one of my friends said, 'You need a brandy.'

I thought I probably looked like I could do with one, but I told her I didn't drink. 'I wasn't talking to you,' she laughed. 'I was talking to my sister.'

The thing was, that night I was tempted to have a drink, but I didn't. I stuck to the 7-Up. In all my life, I have never needed alcohol to have fun, and it was always either water or soft drinks for me.

For so long, I never felt that Spirit really thought I was of any value. So why were these things happening to me now? There was no reason to be singled out like that. None at all. And to be honest, I was just embarrassed by the things that had happened to me. How could I explain it to anyone when I didn't know what was going on myself?

Regarding my falling in spirits, some were saying that I was "chosen", but I thought that was a bit OTT if you understand what I mean. I was just Catherine from Ballybunion. I had been invisible all of my life and no one knew how much at that moment I wanted to run and hide. Being at the centre of attention did not really suit me.

I thought it was strange that there are saintly people in the world who work tirelessly for Spirit, helping the poor, the sick and the lonely, and yet they haven't had experiences like mine—or if they did, they weren't exposed by Spirit in the same way I was. I am most definitely not one of these saintly souls, just someone struggling through life doing ordinary things in her ordinary world. Then I recalled the words in the Bible, 'Blessed are those who do not see, and yet believe.' Maybe I needed proof that God was real.

After all, He had not protected me when I was a child and through all those traumatic incidents when I was attacked by evil in various forms. When I was in trouble, when I needed Him, He did not seem to be there. Maybe I'd given up on God at some level without realising it. But yet, here I was with my world turned upside down and inside out in the space of a few months. Maybe I was one of His lost sheep and He decided to find me. But did He have to do it so publicly?

Once again text from the Bible came to mind. The parable of the prodigal son related to the story of a farmer who had two sons. One son took his share of the fortune, went away and partied like there was no tomorrow, while the other one went out and diligently worked in the fields. Since his brother had abandoned the farm, he probably assumed everything would be his one day. The wayward brother had a right royal time of wine, women and song till eventually, his money ran out.

He went and hired himself out as a swineherd, a menial job that saw him always hungry. At times, he even ate the pigs' food out of their trough. After some time, while wallowing in self-pity, he remembered what it was like to live in his father's house with his family and friends and how good life was back then, even for the least of his servants. And there he was now, gaunt and bedraggled, eating slop and sleeping rough.

He eventually decided to go back home and ask his father if he could be a servant. When he came close to the house his father saw him and started running towards him. Rather than being on the receiving end of any angry tirade, the prodigal son was warmly embraced by his father. Full of remorse, the son suggested he could be his father's servant and work for him in his house but his father, with tears rolling down his cheeks, said, 'You are my son, you've come home. I have so longed for this day.'

So the fatted calf was killed and a wild and happy celebration ensued. There was only one at the party who felt put out, his brother. He could not understand why his dad was so happy to have his errant son home. It was only after his father took him aside and said the following words to him that he understood. 'Son, you are always with me,' the father said, 'and all that is mine is yours. But it was fitting to celebrate and be glad because this brother of yours was dead and is alive again; he was lost and is found.'

As I write about the story, I see it as a metaphor for the forgiveness of God who, with open arms, welcomes us home to Him, regardless of what we have done in life. I certainly did not live a life of partying and hedonism, but I *was* lost and had lived through a time in my life when my faith was challenged. I believe God gives up on no one and would do anything He could to show His love for us, His children, without interfering with the gift of free will He gave us.

Maybe the Father was trying to save me from the depths of my despair by leaving me in no doubt that He was involved in my spiritual journey. Maybe this was His version of coming to meet me. He had, through these recent happenings, thrown me a lifeline and a challenge.

Believe in the light, not darkness. Believe in good, not evil, and you will find your way home. There is no escaping God's love. For sure, my journey would have been a lot easier if I hadn't been affected by the trauma and evil that shaped the earlier part of my life. It is not always easy to hold onto love and light in the face of so many battles. But I know now that in the presence of light, darkness has no real power and God's love will always shine through.

If anyone thought that God coming into my life the way He did signalled an easy ride for me that would be far from the truth. Life was still going to have its challenges. At the time, there I was, still in the throes of motherhood. James, my son, was a teenager—and a very active one—and Nora was eleven. And between Tony and myself, we tried to keep going and deal with whatever problems came our way.

I really believe that no one escapes challenges, no one gets a free ride. Having children was not simple for me, but I have to say after the trouble and traumas I went through it has been a blessing to see my children thrive. As with all families, we have had our struggles but life keeps going, as it always does. Gradually, I started to accept the challenges in my life with more and more gratitude.

God and the angels moved a lot nearer to me and my world, from being on the periphery of my everyday life to being so much in my thoughts, actions and feelings. Spirituality became more important to me than it had ever been before. I had no idea where my path was going to lead, but I knew deep inside my whole being things were changing, and I would be looked after. I would be safe as the new road ahead opened up little by little, and I was aware that all I had to do was travel the journey one step at a time.

There is a Buddhist saying, 'Before enlightenment, chop wood, draw water and after enlightenment, chop wood, draw water.' Even though I had these amazing experiences I still lived an ordinary life. That's what any of us should do: keep living our human existence.

Ultimately, I believe this is all we can do. When God wants us to spiritually wake up, I do feel that we can be pushed by Him until our soul screams from the depth of our being: pay attention, see the truth, God is here. God was always here, but only now we are more aware of Him. With this knowledge, the choices and the realisation of His reality it is easier to make the right choices based on honesty and integrity.

I continued to attend the Padre Pio Masses whenever they were held in the church. Then one day, out of the blue, the local priest asked me to be a witness, to tell my story to the congregation. At first, I wasn't sure I wanted to because I had never spoken in front of an audience before. But then I looked at it from a different perspective: it was not just a new experience for me, it was a privilege to be asked to bear witness to these experiences of Spirit. If I could not say a few words for God, then what would I do if I was asked to make a real sacrifice? So with a certain amount of fear and trepidation I agreed, I said yes, I would speak, and I would bear witness.

But you know the way you agree to something and then suffer the consequences of your actions? Its fine until the realisation dawns that there is no way out of this. You're going to have to stand up and be counted. If I hadn't had time to think about it, I would have been OK, but I did, and became quite anxious. I repeatedly asked myself, *What have I agreed to?* I was to talk In front of a church full of people! I also worried about superficial things like whether I should get a new outfit or new shoes or get a new hairdo. The whole issue gave me many sleepless nights, I can tell you, as I worried about everything from stage fright through to the possibility of no one turning up on the night.

Eventually, the day came, and there I stood in the church in front of a large congregation. My nerves were jangling, and I wasn't sure if I would be able to get the words out of my mouth. Suddenly, I found myself talking about the day I nearly drowned, when Padre Pio first came to my aid and told me I would be OK, and how I was rescued by Father Galvin. I also told the congregation that over the years, I had experienced several spiritual encounters and that during some of those times, my spirit momentarily left my body. I also mentioned the painful moments in my life, when I was depressed, angry and hurt and felt that God could have given me more help when I needed it. As I talked, I was aware that you could hear a pin drop.

People were really listening. The whole thing was quite extraordinary. It was like I was saying things that struck a chord with those present, things that many people probably felt at some periods in their lives: abandonment, isolation and loneliness.

A few days before my talk I decided to prepare properly for the evening. I sat down and spent ages writing out my speech. When I walked into the church armed with my sheets of paper, my plan was to read from my written script. But just before I stood up to go to the podium I looked at my speech and saw to my astonishment that the words on the sheets of paper had just disappeared. God was at it again, embarrassing me. Somehow I knew I wasn't being let read from what I'd written. I was on my own—or was I?

Amazingly, I did not panic. I knew I had to completely trust and when I did, that was when the words just came to me. I should have known that there was no need to be afraid. I found myself talking to everyone with an easy fluency and purpose. It almost felt like it wasn't me, and all of a sudden I realised that the angels were helping me. What a wonderful thing.

As I spoke with clarity and calmness, I could feel the angels gently channelling healing words through me. God hadn't abandoned me at all. He had just taken away the crutches of prepared speech and demonstrated that all I needed was to trust and have faith in Him. It was a real lesson of letting go and letting God.

I even brought humour into what I was saying. The priest was laughing as well and enjoying the messages that were coming through me from Spirit. When I finished speaking the priest came over and thanked me. I was so happy and relieved. Then everyone else wanted to shake hands with me and thank me for bearing witness. In my heart, I was saying, *Silly me, I should have known that the angels and God would have looked after me.*

I asked a friend who came to support me what she thought about the speech, and she said I was just amazing. She said she never knew I could speak so well and clearly. To be honest, I was a bit overwhelmed and nonplussed by the amount of interest people had in what I had talked about. But whatever transpired that night, I knew that it was all divinely guided.

Yes, I was the person speaking those words, but really it was all down to God, Padre Pio and the angels. I had no doubt about that. I thought to myself, from here on in, it might be a good idea to let them take the lead.

I have to say back then I didn't believe in myself very much but now I know that through God, all things are possible. Miracles can happen. I didn't know much about real spirituality, like what to do when my spirit left my body—and I can tell you it's really something. From all the amazing encounters with Spirit I had at the church, I became renewed and reawakened, and much closer to God and the angels.

Every time Spirit interferes in your life, it is a challenge. We are used to living our lives in our own worlds, trying to do all the day-to-day things in life that we are meant to do, because we simply have no choice. We do our best and battle against negativity, pain, and hurt, but unfortunately we can get bogged down by life and think that criticism, anger and frustration are the norm rather than joy, laughter and celebration. In fact, most of the time life is like the Irish weather. One day, you have the sun, the next day rain and the next day a mixture of the two. But we need it all so that life can flourish.

In most belief systems, we are taught that God and the angels watch over us and guide us. The religious teachings say that if you need help you can ask the angels or saints, and if assistance is meant to come to you, it won't pass you by. But the problem is that sometimes you want your life to be the way *you* want it to be. You want the angels to give you the life and answers you want the way *you* want them, but God's plan is always better than yours, and you must learn to believe this. Eventually, you will die and go back to God and one day you will understand your own unique journey and the need for it to have been just the way it was.

But for now, you just have to trust and believe. One day you'll be free from the Earth and its thinking and even if you think you did not do your best, I believe you will see it all from a different perspective on the other side. You will have a wonderful home in heaven because God loves you. Your own guilt, resentment and bitterness is what stops you enjoying God's love here.

Padre Pio reached out and healed a lot of people when he walked the earth, and so I suppose it stands to reason that God would allow him to do some of what he did on Earth from Spirit now, so as to continue his good work. I am sure, with his newfound freedom in spirit, Pio continues his devotion and service.

For whatever reason, he took an interest in a little girl drowning in the sea off Ballybunion in Ireland. Mind you, I wouldn't say he knew anything about Ballybunion when he was alive and living in Italy! I believe he has been around my life for a long time and has helped me through difficult and traumatic experiences, even when I was so low that I lost touch with the spirit world. I feel very privileged and grateful that he is still looking after me to this day, and also to know I was never alone.

It is now eleven years since those first experiences of fallings in spirit, and I am still a regular visitor at the Padre Pio Masses in Lixnaw. It's where I feel safest and most supported, and I feel Padre Pio likes me to spend time there too. Whenever I sit in stillness and peace, surrounded by fellow pilgrims, I receive a real nourishment of the spirit and that gives me peace and courage to keep moving ahead to wherever God may lead me in the future.

Chapter 14
Spiritual Development

I have heard of many people who talked about wonderful healing they got simply by being at Padre Pio Masses, and now I was one of them. At these masses, a scent of roses and sacred incense have often been detected and is a sign that Padre Pio's spirit is present. People sometimes see lights on the altar as well. A framed relic of one of Padre Pio's gloves is occasionally displayed and has been known to give blessings to those needing healing of mind, body or spirit. All these things show that the saint is still serving God and people today and is helping humanity just as much as he did when he was in San Giovanni.

Through today's wonderful priests and dedicated followers of Padre Pio, the world keeps moving forward with this holy man's spiritual love and support which touched so many people during his lifetime. San Giovanni itself has become a major centre of pilgrimage for people from all over the world who have a deep abiding faith in the little monk.

There are still so many things I have to learn spiritually with regard to my own hopes and expectations. Of course, these are often only understood in hindsight. For example, after a few experiences of falling in spirit and other spiritual incidents, it got to the stage that if I went to the church and nothing happened I'd be a bit disappointed! I'd wonder had Padre Pio and the angels forgotten about me. I suppose at some level I was looking for even more proof of the truth of my experiences, and further evidences that little Catherine from Ballybunion really mattered.

I suppose it was all about being human. I know now that this can be a problem for Spirit. If someone gets too much proof or affirmation, they may continue to seek further evidence, to be entertained and boost their sense of self-importance rather than learn, trust and surrender. They have to learn to accept with humility that all spiritual experiences are gifts from Spirit.

The truth is: God, the angels and holy spirits like Padre Pio are always with us—just a thought away. At times, they sit quietly in the background; then at other times, they grace us with spectacular moments. All we have to do is know that if it is right for us, they will show themselves, talk to us or just make their presence felt, and if it's not, they won't show themselves. I often feel spirits around me: a touch at my face, a gentle caress, a whisper, a breath. I'm sure a lot of people do.

They may not always be angels and saints; they could be loved ones who have passed into spirit. These little moments from the other side can bring great comfort and reassurance to anyone sad or grieving. There is no doubt that love transcends the grave, and experiences like this show us there is no separation.

The priests who have hosted the Padre Pio Masses across Ireland and beyond are very dedicated men. The ones I came across in Lixnaw have a great sense of humour and time in the church just flew by because the ceremonies were so celebratory and positive. These priests, always ready for a song or a tale, never behaved like they were religious elite. I felt treated like I belonged.

I was part of one great family. When someone opens their hearts like that to you, it's infectious, and you feel inspired to pass on their positivity and kindness to others. I have to say I felt the love and warmth just grow and grow.

An older priest who regularly came to Lixnaw shared stories of Padre Pio's good works, miracles and healings. On one particular evening, this lovely soul was a co-celebrant of the Mass. When I went up to Communion I noticed that his gaze became focused on me. As this happened, I felt a strange sensation. It was like I experienced a son of mystical connection with this man.

Another priest who happened to be nearby saw my restlessness and told me, 'Be calm, it's Communion time.' Sometime later, when I knew a bit more about spiritual matters, I realised that my spirit somehow has the ability to elevate at very special spiritual moments or times of high spiritual intensity. My restlessness was my physical body trying to keep my spirit grounded.

A few days later a friend asked me if I could hold some kind of fundraising event for her child, who needed an operation. She lived in Duagh, a village about ten miles away from Lixnaw, and she said she thought their church grounds might be a suitable venue. Of course, I said I would—what mother could refuse a request like that? As I considered what I could do, the answer came to me. A crystal sale!

I had always loved crystals and minerals, and I knew I could get crystals on sale and return from a contact of mine. I was also delighted that the crystals would be sold for a very good cause. I told my friend my idea, and she thought that would be great. I contacted the priest in Duagh, and he kindly gave me permission to set up a display stand in the church grounds.

It might be considered strange to sell crystals at a church, but many people forget that crystals have often been mentioned in the Bible. One instance was when God instructed King Solomon to create a shield for himself. He directed the king to use several specific crystals for the construction of the shield so that he could be protected. If we could only understand the full extent of God's gifts! There is nothing on this Earth that has come into being but by His gracious hands. So whenever you see people using crystals for healing these days, know that they are using the gifts that God created when he made this beautiful planet.

Using what God has created in nature is not opposed to God, it actually shows gratitude to Him. In today's world of modem medicine, crystals and minerals are regularly used. We also use crystals for practical purposes, for example, quartz is used in watches and in mobile phones.

The day I arrived in Duagh to set up the table it was pelting down with rain. The priest was there waiting for me and invited me into the church for a cup of tea and cake before I set up. I have to say I was touched by his kindness and generosity. As we chatted, I told him about my spiritual experiences, and he was tremendously interested and keen to know all about my connection with God, the angels and Padre Pio. I was so pleasantly surprised by his openness and acceptance of me, and felt very much at ease with this wonderfully spiritual man.

Then we set up the crystals together, and between the two of us, we made quite a few euros for the fund, which was great. The day ended as it had begun, with rain. I certainly got damp on that soft Kerry day, but I didn't mind because the whole event had been such a positive experience.

After that day, I learned that projection is a bad thing. Sometimes we may think that older priests are more formal and conservative. The priest I met that day was not young but was very open and inclusive, and I have found that there are in fact many of those who choose service as a way of life. So it is important that we meet people with openness and not prejudice, and know that we are all God's children.

A couple of weeks later, at another Padre Pio Mass, I was sitting on the far left side of a pew in the church. It was just before the ceremony began. All of a sudden I felt something invisible pushing me, moving me towards the middle of the bench where I would be directly in line with the priest giving the service. I guessed it was the angels at work. For some reason, I thought this was so funny that I was compelled to laugh.

Before I knew it, people got caught up in my mirth and began laughing themselves. Pretty soon the whole church was laughing with no one knowing what they were laughing at. To be honest, it was a great way to start the Mass. Honestly, sometimes I think the angels are like bold children and enjoy setting me up at times! They certainly had the last laugh that day, as all I kept hearing during the Mass was Padre Pio's voice saying: *You have to go to San Giovanni with the priest on the altar on the pilgrimage that is being arranged.*

All I knew about Padre Pio at that stage was that he had appeared to me in Ballybunion and saved me from drowning, and he was a kindly-looking monk with holes in his hands and feet. I didn't know they were called stigmata for a number of years. I also didn't know he was a mystic or a healer and could levitate and bilocate. I eventually researched him and found out Padre Pio had died eight years before my drowning incident. Then it hit me that I had actually seen a dead person. And after that I wondered how many other dead people had I seen over the years unbeknownst to myself?

And now here was Padre Pio telling me to go to San Giovanni, which had been his home in Italy. When spiritual events first started happening to me in the church I promised I would go visit his home at some point in the future as a sort of thank you. Now I was being clearly nudged at the Mass by Padre Pio's voice frequently reminding me, '*I am with you, and it is time to visit me.*' He had always been near me when I really needed him and now this seemed to be the start of a new journey for me.

I found out that Padre Pio's spirit regularly appears to people who are ill and call on him for help. When someone is sick or is in hospital he is often there assisting and reassuring patients that all is well and in divine order. It is obviously a source of great comfort for people in those situations.

Healing comes in many forms. Some people see healing only as being cured from an illness, or being kept alive. Of course, some people do heal and get better, which is wonderful. But then there also are sick people who, no matter how much loved ones pray for them, do not get better and who pass away. Those who have prayed for them may become angry because they think their prayers haven't been answered or God and whoever else they prayed to hasn't been listening to them.

But that's not correct. The prayers are always heard, and each person is healed according to what they need. There is huge healing in dying as it is an end to suffering and pain and the start of a new life in heaven. That is why Padre Pio has said, 'Pray, hope and don't worry. Worry is useless. God is merciful and will hear your prayer.'

If you're not meant to be here on Earth past a certain time and date, you won't be. Everything is fine, God's always present, and you are not alone. So don't despair when your loved one passes. Grieve but also celebrate their life. If you have called in Spirit, if you have asked for help, then help will be given.

Even if you can't see it, angels attend the bedside of your dying loved one and make the person's passing as safe and as gentle as possible. The person who is dying is well aware of their presence, and any fear they may have about passing dissipates when they see the light of a new dawn and are welcomed home.

Sometimes angels and spirits let you know you are not alone. You could be walking up the street and a stranger stops you and gives you a medal of some angel or saint. It could be something small but whatever it is, it will be recognised as a message specifically for you.

As time has passed, I have almost completely stopped falling in spirit, but still have a few other kinds of spiritual experiences there every now and then. A friend of mine offered the suggestion regarding the fallings in spirit that I was trying to escape my physical life to be with the angels, but was always put back into my body. My friend jokingly added that I haven't been allowed into heaven just yet as I probably would give God a headache talking to Him all the time!

At this point in my life, I was calmer and gentler, and was able to laugh more. Even so, it was still sometimes hard to see who my real friends were, beyond my family. Trust was hard-earned for those even close to me. I had been let down so often and in so many ways. It was hard to remember the bright shining soul I was once, because it was lost among all the hurts and pains of the past.

No wonder I attracted people into my life who would betray me. So even when God came back into my life I didn't accept Him for some time. It was like, Thank you, God, for coming, it's great to see you, but I'm going back behind my walls to Fortress Catherine. My spirit longed for freedom and connection, but my physical being longed for safety and security.

I found myself having talks with God which were quite cathartic. They went something like this: 'God, I am beginning to see what a victim I truly was. Bad things were done to me, and I am not about to let my guard down now or in the future. Some people say the world is an illusion, God. Some illusion.

'I know my two lost babies were real, and I know what the doctors did to me, the pain they caused me. For so long, I have needed to hold on to the pain lest I forget what I have experienced, not to mention the injustice of it all. I have used metaphorical teddy bears to hold onto to protect me from being vulnerable again: one is called Victim, another Anger, another Betrayal, another Abandonment, and another Violation. And I have cried out in the middle of the night in anguish, God. Why did I have to go through all this pain? I am so sad and angry. Here I am now, with my fists up against the world, and you need to understand why.'

There were times when I really did give God an earful. Even though He has touched my life with love it was still going to take time for me to open up from all that I had suffered over the years. I still was here living in the real world, and for most of my life, I did not have choirs of angels singing, nor was I just sitting on fluffy white clouds.

But God and Padre Pio were now showing me I really wasn't lost, and if I opened up, I could feel the light of God placing a balm on my wounds. I could turn my back on God as much as I liked but He would never turn His back on me. At some soul level, I knew the road ahead was not going to be easy, but I knew I was going to heal and that my resurrection was assured.

I also kept hearing in my mind that I needed to work for God, and I knew that staying behind any of my self-made barricades was where darkness wanted me to be, exactly the opposite of where God and Padre Pio wanted me to be. Ships in the harbour are safe, but they are not made to stay in the harbour. Darkness wins when good people do nothing. After much reflection, I decided I was going to fight for all that was good and right. Darkness was not going to win, not on my watch.

There is no doubt that living openly and truthfully can have painful moments, but it is so worth it in the long run. I do believe that God helps those who help themselves, and at that point in my life, I was really trying to move on from past hurts and traumas.

The invitation to San Giovanni I received from Padre Pio would hopefully be another step along the road to my healing. Of course, somehow, I had to go.

Chapter 15
The Pilgrimage

To tell the story of my first visit to San Giovanni and Medjugorje and to expand on my connection with Padre Pio means leaving my own story behind for a moment and focusing on my spiritual journey and the direction it took. Sometimes life moves so fast. It can be like a runaway freight train on steroids. I had come from Kerry in Ireland that makes chill-out an art form. When I made the commitment to Padre Pio to go to San Giovanni, I was not quite sure when or how that would happen. Finances were tight at the time and the country's economy was struggling.

Then in 2014, a church group in Killarney organised a pilgrimage to go to both Medjugorje and San Giovanni and one of our well-loved Padre Pio priests, Father Kevin, who was fondly nicknamed the laughing priest, was going to lead the pilgrimage. He would be accompanied by two other priests who were also devoted to Padre Pio. I know one was from Antrim, but I can't unfortunately remember their names. The overall organiser of the pilgrimage had a great devotion to Padre Pio and actually was following in the footsteps of his mother, who used to organise pilgrimages herself before she passed on the baton to her son. It was to be an eight-day round trip, firstly to visit Medjugorje and the place where six teenagers saw visions of Our Lady, and then to San Giovanni Rotondo where Padre Pio had lived most of his life.

If I had to beg, borrow or steal, I knew I had to be on that trip. Money was always going to be an issue, but I begged my angels to make it happen, and I was full sure they would. I didn't have much money, and it didn't look like I was going to win the lotto any time soon, but I had a feeling deep inside that I was going to go. So with trust and faith in my heart I miraculously managed to scrape together the funds and went and booked myself onto the trip. What a day that was. My heart sang with anticipation.

Even though I knew that a whole group of us were going, I felt it was a very personal gift to me. I could not wait to be on the plane. Still, I suppose it's the same for everyone. On a special trip like this, everyone is on their own very personal journey and will experience things in their own unique way.

For some, it will be the joy of just being in prayer and peaceful meditation. For others, they may hope for healing or strength to endure some difficult challenges. For me, it was the fulfilment of my promise to walk in the footprints of my hero, Pio.

Fifty-one people took the pilgrimage including two friends of mine, each with their own personal hopes and needs. I remember smiling like a Cheshire cat as we boarded the coach that would take us to Dublin Airport. One of my friends travelling with me came from Ennis and the other one was from Kerry. As we travelled, the itinerary was explained to us by those who were hosting the pilgrimage. Every part of the trip was really well-planned, and it looked like we were in for a very busy time! But I was so excited and so ready.

It was almost like the happy anticipation I felt when the Holy Father visited Ireland in 1979. I was like a child let out of school, and it seemed that many of the others felt the same too. The energy was electric. Smiles all round. Everyone was in top form, and it was magic. A few people looked like they had seen it all before, but these were the regular pilgrims, their knees hardened from years of praying, prayer beads at the ready, and serenity and stillness radiating from them.

But not me. For me, everything was fresh and new, a real adventure. I was excited, enthusiastic and happy.

We finally reached Dublin Airport, and within a short space of time, we were boarding the plane, and then we were off. When the plane lifted into the air, so did my heart. I was flying with the angels, leaving Ireland behind and tor those eight days I was just me. Not a mother, a wife, a victim. Just Catherine. At last, I had some sacred space to myself with time to meditate and relax.

We arrived at Split Airport in Bosnia on a beautiful sunny afternoon. It was odd to see armed police patrolling the airport because of course you don't get anything like that in Ireland. The airport itself wasn't that big; to me it was about the size of Cork provincial airport. We boarded a coach and set off on our journey to Medjugorje. After travelling for a while, we stopped at a basic hotel where we stayed one night.

The next morning, after a quick shower and breakfast we resumed our journey. As the road stretched before us, the countryside opened up, and you could see mountains in the distance. I've always loved nature and drank in the beauty of the landscape around me. We actually had to cross two borders to reach our destination.

There was a real party atmosphere as we drove along. We could blame the priests for that! It was clear that they were a “bad” influence on us as they led us in prayer first and sing-songs and stories afterwards. To be honest, we were all so happy to be celebrating life and active spirituality. In Ireland over the years, we had experienced priests who became really involved in their community, and some of them were great singers and dancers. We were really lucky to have these kinds of good-humoured and fun-loving priests with us on this journey.

As a group, we were welcomed everywhere we went. Well, we are Irish, the well-known ambassadors of singing, dancing and having the craic. That said, while we are always known to enjoy fun times we’d never be looking for trouble and had a reputation for being respectful. We generally don’t get too unruly. The people we met in Bosnia and Herzegovina were wonderful.

They were warm, friendly and full of smiles. I thought to myself, we really do find good people all over the world. The locals there made me realise how resilient people can be, considering how much pain their country had suffered in wars and tragedies that had scarred their heritage.

It was late when we arrived at the B&B in Medjugorje. It had been loosely described as a hotel, but I wasn’t disappointed at all. I would have taken this warm and homely place any time over some of the sterile and impersonal modern hotels you get now. We were checked in by a very nice woman and her daughter-in-law. This was to be our base while we were in Medjugorje.

After we had something to eat, my two friends and myself went out for a walk. It was a calm and balmy evening. We were wondering if we could locate St James' church, which is the parish church of Medjugorje. On the way there, somehow I tripped and fell, hurting my knees and elbows. After falling, I decided to go back to the B&B because I was very sore and feeling a bit sorry for myself. My friends were very supportive and decided to come back with me.

In the morning, I felt much better. It was a bright sunny day, and after the three of us had breakfast, we set off for the church, where all of our group were going to meet and attend Mass. We discovered the place was easy enough to find and only a short walk from the B&B. The space outside the church was quite large and filled with rows of benches, along with a raised area where, we were told, outdoor masses were regularly held. At other times, people liked to just sit there and pray and meditate. Also outside the church, surrounded by a little railing, was a lovely white statue of Our Lady.

When we entered the building I looked around and saw the interior was modern, spacious and light-filled. The Mass was given in different languages, and afterwards, we took some time out to wander around and buy a few souvenirs. Then we all set off for Apparition Hill. At the foot of the hill was a blue cross, and we were told that this small area was one of several places of prayer along the way. As we walked up the stony path, we saw a number of bronze images, created by an Italian artist, which represented the Joyful and Sorrowful Mysteries of the Holy Rosary.

Eventually, about halfway up the hill, we came to the place of the apparitions, where we saw a statue of the Queen of Peace, the same statue that was also in front of St James' church. It was a very peaceful spot, and we spent some time there, meditating and praying. For me, these were very special moments, and I soaked up the atmosphere of this very sacred place.

It was about mid-afternoon by the time we made our descent. Going up the stony hill hadn't been easy but coining back down was even harder, and I had to really watch where I was going. I was doing my best to negotiate the terrain when all of a sudden I tripped and fell. I couldn't believe it happened again. It was a strange sensation, actually.

It was almost like something invisible had pushed me. I yelled out, and my friends rushed over to help, bless them. Luckily, I was OK—no broken bones, just some more cuts and bruises to add to the ones I had got the previous evening. I was grateful to lean on my pals as we made our slow descent back to the village. We were all actually in good humour, laughing and giggling about what happened. It would have taken more than a couple of falls to dampen my spirits on this trip!

When we finally arrived back where we were staying, we met up with several others in our group, including the organiser of our trip. When I told him of my fall he said he had learned first aid and went off and got his little kit. As he set about tending to my injuries, he pointed to my feet, and with the coolness and discernment of a surgeon he told me, 'They'll have to go.'

'My toes?' I gasped.

He laughed. 'No silly, the shoes. You will hurt yourself wearing them over here.'

He was right. I was wearing flip flops which were in truth completely unsuitable for rough and stony ground. I decided there and then that they were going to go in the bin. Luckily,

I had also brought my old but trusty runners with me, so they'd now be worn from then on.

Later, at dinner, we chatted with some of the other pilgrims. I was talking to Father Kevin, and he told me that he had actually fallen on Cross Mountain that day, which was located beside Apparition Hill. He had his accident at the same time as me, around three o'clock in the afternoon. What a coincidence, I thought to myself. Father Kevin was intrigued when I brought up the coincidence of our accidents happening at the same time on the same day. We both laughed as we showed each other our cuts and bruises.

He told me he had been to Medjugorje several times and had often climbed the mountain, but had never fallen before. Then he said, 'Let me tell you the story of what happened at 3:00 pm.'

However, he didn't get to tell me as we were interrupted by other people wanting to talk to him. I didn't mind and got into a conversation with another lady. It was actually she who guessed what the priest going to tell me, that Christ died on the cross at three o'clock on Good Friday. Wow. Well, that was certainly something to ponder in my soul. All I can do to this day is be amazed at these unexpected spiritual moments that continue to strengthen my faith, trust and awareness of God in my life.

My bruised brother-in-arms was a very nice man and because he was on my mind I went and bought him a set of rosary beads and got his name inscribed on them. Before we left Medjugofje, I gave him the beads, and he was delighted with them. I told him they were not expensive, and he said it didn't matter. It was the thought that counted. He was a man who was able to receive with a beautiful sense of humility and gratitude.

The next day, a group of us set off to conquer the summit of Cross Mountain. On this climb, a lovely Bosnian lady was going to guide us all the way up to the top. Before we started, I stood there looking up at the mountain. Surrounded by this wide and open landscape on a warm sunny day, I felt swept up in my own world. I wasn't praying, I was just standing there in awe of the beauty of nature all around.

I was so amazed to be present and so grateful that God had brought me to this very special place. Then I suddenly had a vision of myself kneeling down in front of the cross, and as I looked at the imposing structure, it started spinning around and round. I was aware that I was being given knowledge of something that was going to happen in the near future, about how darkness would try to block me from the work I was meant to do. I was to persevere, no matter how difficult things became. At that stage in my life, I was beginning to accept these unusual happenings in my life, instead of trying to rationalise them. There are times, even today, when I see the truth of that message, but I am determined and will keep going as I was asked to do.

The guide started talking just then, and it was her voice which snapped me back to the real world. As we trekked up the mountain, the woman told us that the cross was erected in 1934 in commemoration of the 1,900th anniversary of Jesus' death. She also talked about how Medjugorje was affected by the war in the 1990s, and about the Stations of the Cross which were placed at stages along the way up to the summit. These stations were the Sorrowful Mysteries, the work of the same Italian artist who created the bronze images on

Apparition Hill. The guide then related the story of a priest who died at the third station of the cross—when Jesus fell for the first time—and showed us an engraved stone that had been erected in his memory.

She also spoke about how Mary, the Virgin Mother, visited the children on Apparition Hill and about the many sightings there have been of Our Lady in the area ever since. As I trod up the mountain, I lifted a pebble to take with me as a memento of walking on this sacred ground and the privilege it was to be there.

At the top of the mountain, I spent some time checking to see if there was a button or a switch that could cause the cross to spin around. I asked the guide, who just laughed at the idea. I did accept the vision I received was real, but I am human too and wanted to verify that the phenomenon I experienced hadn't been man-made or was just my imagination.

And so yes, that did verify it for me and removed any doubt I may have had. Furthermore, on that day I talked to a lot of other walkers, and it was heart-warming to hear several stories about pilgrims who had also experienced profound encounters with God and Our Lady in the mountains and in the churches in Medjugorje. It was clear I was just one of many having special experiences as I journeyed on my pilgrimage.

Back in my little room in the B&B, I wrote my recollections and thoughts about the memorable day.

As I sit here in the evening, as my time in Medjugorje comes to a close, I find some quiet space to just stop and ponder how my life has been up to now and how it is all now starting to make sense. I have real hope that the pain I suffered had a purpose and that life may be better from here on in. I am now starting to get some space from the rollercoaster of disasters that blighted my younger life and to review and re-evaluate my thinking. Here, in the stillness, I realise that a new me is emerging with a future I never knew could exist.

A new day is dawning full of hope and faith, and I feel that my future has a real sense of promise and purpose. I know I can be in touch with the spirit world and can hear spirits. I've also always had a special connection to Mary our Mother, and have carried her name since birth. I've been to Knock on many occasions and walked around the area where Mary appeared with Jesus to people in the heart of rural Ireland at a time when hope was really needed. I truly believe that is why they appeared in the first place: to let people know that even in the depths of life's struggles, we are never alone. Angels and spirits are always with us.

I have been thinking how difficult it must have been for Mary, the mother of Jesus, to see her beautiful Son on the cross. I know that is how she understands mothers and their pain at a very deep and personal level. But it must have been wonderful then after His resurrection to see her child once again and see the true purpose of His life in the world of spirit. I know I'll feel the joy of connecting with Michael and Lizzy again when I pass over. I will understand why my journey was as it was, and in doing so, the pain and sadness I have carried throughout my life on Earth will be gone and replaced with happiness and celebration.

I know and believe the life of Jesus was not about the suffering of crucifixion, but the joy of resurrection. He died to give us faith and hope and to release us from despair. He experienced crucifixion to help birth a new world, and He did it all for us. I think also of how, in our own journeys through life, we experience being put down, criticised, not believed in, belittled, and told we're not good enough. These are messages of darkness and do not represent truth.

For myself, I see an invitation to resurrect ourselves daily. 'This is the Day the Lord has made. I will rejoice and be glad.' In recent times, I have been told that I have helped people a lot, but the highest compliment I could ever have received was to be told I was one of God's children and an integral part of his great big family.

Darkness often comes with an excuse and a negative calling to be less than we are, while light often comes with a challenge and a loving invitation to see we are greater than we thought we could ever be. To perform a random kindness touches a heart, helps a soul and raises our vibration. As I sit here tonight, I want to do what is asked of me, God.

My heart reaches out to the people of Medjugorje. These kind and gentle people are living, by some standards, a very basic existence, but their simple needs and peace are tremendous gifts and are an example to us all. Life and living can be joyful and rewarding if we don't get consumed with material desires and stresses, and instead learn to go with the flow of life.'

The following day our group would move on to San Giovanni Rotondo in Italy. I promised Our Lady I would come back someday to Medjugorje, and I asked her to look after my little angels in heaven and my children here on Earth. I knew my past was slowly but definitely mending and a brighter future now lay before me, with my spirit lightening and reaching towards faith, hope, peace and happiness.

Chapter 16
Place of My Dreams

It's funny, but I sometimes feel a bit precious about Padre Pio because he is, for me, a treasured protector, guide and teacher. He helped many people during his life, and even more after he passed into Spirit, and I am sure he will continue to do so. I look forward to meeting him in person when I join him in heaven. He helped me believe there is a divine purpose to my life and that I needed to survive my traumas, learn from them and know that every tomorrow is a new day. In all those moments of spiritual help, I felt so privileged and supported.

As I began to find my way through the darkness, I wasn't sure for a while how to reach out to people, so I could be of assistance to them. I worried that I was not good enough to be of service to the divine and found myself asking God, 'Are you sure you have the right person? I'm just Catherine O'Connor from Ballybunion. I'm the one to whom the teacher in school said I would never do anything with my life.'

From an early age, there was always a restlessness and edginess about me. I always had to be on the go. I can understand why my teacher found it hard to teach me, as my mind was often anywhere but on my lessons. Now I know why. I was like a ball of energy waiting for direction and longing to escape the mundane, but at the time, I was unprepared to listen to people.

I was always destined to do it my way, or so I thought. Imagine, it must have taken a whole team of higher beings, with the fine art of gentle persuasion, to keep me on track. As I thought this I heard, *'You're right Mary, a very large team,'* and a huge laugh. *'The Blessed Virgin, Archangel Michael, Padre Pio, a host of angels and saints and many more besides in Heaven and Earth—but you'll get there eventually.'*

We left Medjugorje with many of us promising to return another time. Our coach then took us on a long journey through amazing countryside baked in beautiful sunshine, the weather a far cry from the rain and drizzle of my home in Kerry. We travelled through Bosnia and Croatia, and I vaguely remember going by broad expanses of fields and mountains and rivers and many small villages and towns. With each mile that passed, I could feel my excitement building. I still could hardly believe I was going to finally visit the place of my dreams.

My mind and spirit danced with my imagination, and my thoughts ran ahead of me to this wonderful place I was sure would be a piece of heaven. My friends knew I was away in my own world and kindly let me be. They joined in with all the singing, laughter, prayer and storytelling that went on all the time in our bus of happy pilgrims.

In Ireland, some people have dubbed me Scary Mary from Tipperary, even though I'm from Kerry. It is a name I earned because I can be quite direct in my approach. I think that after this trip, they could have called me Fairy Mary because I was definitely away with the fairies as I travelled to the home of my hero by land and by sea. I felt my heart and spirit had already been in residence in San Giovanni for some time, and I anticipated feeling a great sense of completion when I finally got there physically.

Eventually, we arrived at Split where we took a ferry across the Adriatic Sea to Ancona in Italy. Then we drove southwards, stopping about half an hour later to visit the Sanctuary of the Holy House of Loreto. Legend has it that Our Lady's house, the house where the Annunciation took place, was transported to the hill of Loreto, not by modern means, but by God and His angels.

Apparently, technology has confirmed that the building materials and techniques used in the stonework are the same as those used in the Holy Land. However, although it is a famous shrine I did not feel a great connection to the place. I guess it was because any focus I had was by then on our final destination, the home of Saint Pio.

From Loreto, we travelled on down to Monte Sant'Angelo and to the monastery and sanctuary of St Matthew, where a relic from this apostle rests. We all received a very warm welcome from the monks and were given time to look around this wonderful place. During the visit, I bought some holy oil, so I can say I wasn't away with the fairies all the time! There I felt I was walking in the footsteps of ancient pilgrims, and I would really like to go back there again sometime.

We all got back on the bus once more and arrived in San Giovanni at around seven o'clock in the evening. After booking into our hotel, we came down for dinner, which was very pleasant, and then myself and the girls went for a walk. I couldn't wait to get out the door and experience the place. My spirits were high, but as I ventured out of the hotel and looked around, I saw to my great disappointment that my romantic vision of a village in the mountains was dashed. San Giovanni was a far cry from what I had imagined.

It was quite a modern place, totally unlike the rural village of Medjugorje, and several streets were reminiscent of Moore Street in Dublin on market day. Padre Pio statues, medals, plates, key rings, you name it, all kinds of religious souvenirs were for sale everywhere. Some of the statues were OK but most were just marginally representative of my hero, and a lot of them were not from Italy. They were foreign imports. Whoever made them, they sure as heck didn't get his best side.

I was waiting for one of the sellers to shout: 'Padre Pios, two for the price of one, get your Padre Pios here, Padre Pios going cheap, if you don't want him don't maul him.' The unexpected stench of commercialism tore at my soul. I was dismayed and saddened at the display of so much hard business and cheap profit around me.

My Padre Pio was never about opulence and wealth. He lived a simple spiritual life, and here was his town now almost smothered by commercialism and trade. I remembered Saint Matthew's gospel when Christ went to the temple and became angry at the people trading in the sacred grounds of God's house. I imagined for a brief moment losing the plot and giving it out to the vendors around me. Then I took a deep breath, and told myself, 'Calm down, calm down! You'd only be arrested and spend time in an Italian jail.'

I could nearly see the headlines: 'Kerry pilgrim goes berserk in San Giovanni!' I took control of myself and continued strolling with my friends who were in grand form chatting away and happily looking around at all and sundry. They were oblivious to my disappointment at my expectations not being met and just enjoying the experience of being in the moment and seeing what was new for them. Because they did not have any expectations, they celebrated while I mourned.

I am an explorer. When I go somewhere I like to see the place's architecture and art. I also like to see people, how they live, the colour and culture of a place. I love to get a sense of where I am, to feel the energy of the land and those who live there. I do not sit still. I mosey around and take it all in, but because I was so thrown by this place being a busy modern town instead of a beautiful little Italian village, I was quite unsettled and agitated.

I tried to rationalise it, that God can be found in towns as well as small villages. And then Spirit reminded me of the message I received back in Ireland: *You have to go to San Giovanni.* I knew this was not a holiday, and that I was here to meet Padre Pio in his sacred home. But I still couldn't find peace within myself. My illusions were shattered.

Medjugorje really had been so beautiful in every way, whereas San Giovanni left me with a sense of sorrow. I began to realise that I had a view that the simple life was a spiritual life, and it was impossible to be spiritual in a place that was full of hustle and bustle. Deep inside I knew I had to let go of prejudices like this, but as we continued our stroll, a great wave of grief and sadness overtook me. Even as I experienced the sensation, I felt it was crazy for something like this to affect Rile this way.

After all, in Ireland, we have Knock, and there are religious artefacts sold in many shops there, and I readily accepted them, so why was I having such a terrible problem? It didn't take away the sacredness of Knock for me in any way. Our Lady was definitely in residence there. Had I some idea that I was in a world of my own creation where I had ownership over Padre Pio and no one else was allowed to have him?

Then I noticed that the people in the shops and on the streets were warm and friendly, and when I looked up at the countryside surrounding us, I saw it was actually very nice. I had read the town was located on the slopes of Monte Calvo, and as I scanned the scenery, I could see lots of greenery adorning the hills in the distance. I kept telling myself I had a tremendous amount to be grateful for, and I was privileged to be there—and yet…

My pals and I eventually turned around and headed back to the hotel for a well-earned rest. I think I might have walked them around a bit too much, but there was a lot to see. Since it was a lovely evening I decided to go and sit outside in the hotel grounds by myself, and just be.

Finally, on my own, I burst into tears. The tears were uncontrollable. I felt I was being silly, but I could not stop crying. A few minutes later, I saw Father Kevin, who was apparently taking some quiet time out in the balmy air as well. He spotted me and came over. His friendly expression changed to concern when he saw I was upset. I could feel his compassion reach out to me.

'Why are you crying, Catherine?' he asked.

Wiping my tears, I blurted out, 'This place is too commercial! Padre Pio would not like that, he wouldn't. He was a sacred holy man more interested in people than in product and profit.'

Father Kevin said he saw where I was coming from, and that he had seen that reaction before, many times, from other pilgrims.

‘Not everyone believes that the spiritual and commercial can go hand in hand,’ he said.

I replied, ‘I haven’t seen too much evidence of the spiritual in the Padre Pio statues and memorabilia, not to mention the price of them. Some of them look quite cheap and nasty, and some of the pictures of him could be more tasteful.’

‘I understand,’ Father Kevin agreed, ‘but hold your judgements till tomorrow. Then I’ll show you the real San Giovanni, where you can experience the heart of Padre Pio, and where you will be able to celebrate your favourite saint. In that sacred place, you’ll see the locations in which he lived and worked and where he was laid to rest.’

He gave me a tissue and said, ‘Come on now. Let’s have no more tears. Just celebrate life and the fact that you are here. I have been to San Giovanni many times before, and I always feel I am blessed whenever I come here, and that I can live my life in divine service. Let yourself find joy surrendering to the gift you’ve been given by coming to this wonderful place.’

Father Kevin’s kind and considerate words sank home, and I felt a bit lighter. He was right. I needed to trust and believe in God’s guidance and that there was a lot more to being here than I had experienced up to now. Later, I went to bed with a little more hope than before of what I might possibly experience the following day.

Chapter 17
The Sanctuary

When I woke up in San Giovanni the next morning I felt different. Gone was the sense of loss I'd experienced the evening before, replaced by a deep feeling of gratitude for being there. I had left my prejudices behind and felt more hopeful and optimistic about what was to come on this part of the journey. Father Kevin's support and gentle encouragement, along with his suggestion to find the real reason I was here, helped me stay positive.

After breakfast, Father Kevin told us what the visit to Padre Pio's shrine would entail. We would first go to the English Office where we would see a DVD about the saint's life and works. Then we would go to Mass, and after that, we would go down to the crypt which housed Padre Pio's remains. We would then have free time to wander and explore and didn't have to be back at the hotel until 7:00 pm for dinner. Father Kevin reminded us that everyone in San Giovanni took a siesta from about 12 midday until about 5:00 pm as it was too hot to work during those hours. Then after the meal, we would be free again for the rest of the evening.

So out we all went, eager to start this special day. The documentary about Padre Pio was engrossing and captivating, and we all enjoyed it. I think a brief summary of his life is worth recounting here.

This holy man's life was incredible and his great works have helped so many people throughout the years. From a young age, he saw visions and knew early on that he wanted to devote his life to God. When he was sixteen he joined the novitiate order of the Capuchin Friars in Sant'Angelo, and it was there he took the name of Friar Pio. In 1910, he was ordained a priest, and in 1911, he received the first stigmata on his hands and feet. They were not permanent at that time, and even though he experienced Christ's pain deeply, they were not visible to the naked eye.

It was only in August 1918 when they appeared again that they remained as open visible wounds, until his death. In September 1918, another mystical event happened to him. He was saying confession when a heavenly being came and threw a fire-tipped spear at him. According to Padre Pio, he felt a horrific pain in his heart, but in time he came to understand that the experience was a gift from God. This phenomenon is actually called transverberation. The injury caused by the being left a wound on Padre Pio's side in the shape of an X.

After hearing about his mystical experiences, many didn't believe Padre Pio and actually denounced him, and the religious authorities went on to ban him from all of his ministry, except for Mass, for two years. Eventually, things calmed down, and he resumed all his priestly duties. He became so popular that sometimes he had to say Mass outside the church, as there was not enough room inside to hold all the pilgrims.

Padre Pio suffered from poor health his entire life but offered up his illnesses as a sacrifice to God for the conversion of souls. Even though he was endowed with many spiritual gifts, he was a humble man and said he never felt worthy of them. His whole life was filled with prayer, celebrating Mass and hearing confessions, and his usual workday was around nineteen hours. One of the pieces of advice he used to give people was, 'Pray, hope and don't worry. Anxiety does not help at all. Our merciful Lord will listen to our prayers.'

Many miracles have been attributed to Padre Pio during and after his life, but the saint himself always urged people to thank God, who is the source of all miracles. He was also able to see into people's hearts and spent many hours of the day in the confessional.

Furthermore, through the gift of bilocation, Padre Pio was sometimes able to be in different places at the same time, to help and heal people.

You know the phrase, 'By their fruits ye shall know them?' Well, if Padre Pio's works are anything to go by, he really is a saint by his deeds as well as by his holiness. One thing I greatly admired about him was how grounded he was. He had his time and space for meditation, but he remained absolutely present when he needed to be. It was in 1947, with the help of devotees the world over, that he started building the huge House of Relief of Suffering Hospital, one brick at a time.

He was adamant the building would not be built with borrowed money. He knew God would provide. And if the funding ever stopped, the building would stop as well. His trust and faith were such that construction never ceased and the money needed was always there.

Building was completed in 1956 and this hospital is now recognised as one of the most advanced scientific research hospitals in Europe. It is also considered one of Padre Pio's great legacies. His thinking around the whole project, from the start, was clear and direct and his intention very focused.

He died on 22nd September 1968 at the age of eighty-one. At that stage, the poor man suffered from severe arthritis and used a wheelchair most of the time. He was given the Last Rites and his final words were, 'Jesus, Mary.'

I was only six years of age when Padre Pio made his transition into spirit. Even so, I feel honoured by the fact that I was walking the earth at least some of the time as my hero.

After the documentary, Father Kevin led us over to the sanctuary. The whole area was amazing and very impressive. The large churchyard in front of the church and shrine is bordered by twelve fountains symbolising the River Jordan, and on the north side of the churchyard are twenty-four olive trees representing the twelve prophets and twelve apostles of Christ. We walked over to a row of large stone bells and a crucifix, and were told by one of the priests that each bell was dedicated to a saint from the order of Franciscan Friars.

As our group stood around in this place for a few moments, I suddenly heard the bells play sweet, beautiful music. Impossible, I thought, these bells can't move. Then I realised that I must be hearing these sounds on a spiritual level. I focused more, and to my surprise, I recognised the music as a hymn I knew from my childhood called "The Bells of the Angelus".

But that hymn never sounded as beautiful as it did in those few sacred moments. It was magical. I was in awe as I listened to it. Then our group moved towards the church entrance, and as we did, the music gently faded away. I don't know if anyone else had the same experience, but I definitely know what I heard.

`This massive modem shrine and church dedicated to Padre Pio can hold up to 6,500 people, with standing room for 30,000 people outside. It was built because there was just not enough room in the original church, Santa Maria delle Grazie, to hold all the thousands of pilgrims that come to San Giovanni on a daily basis. On the front side of the church is a huge stained glass window, featuring details of the Apocalypse of St John. The crypt is also within the grounds of this church.

The Mass was lovely and was attended by a large crowd. When it was over we went over to a ramp and down steps to a curving walkway which would take us to the crypt. I believe you can also access the crypt from the churchyard outside. As we walked along, I felt the sacredness in this space, and the sounds and atmosphere of the town faded into the background. Those extraneous noises lost their significance, and all that was left was incredible and beautiful stillness. Both sides of the walkway were lined with scenes made from mosaics which depicted various events from Padre Pio's life.

As we entered the crypt, I saw the ceiling was made of gold and ceramic tiles, which gave the low-lit room a celestial glow. The gold was donated by people who were grateful for the privilege of being there. This place was actually another church, and ahead of rows of wooden seats was an altar where priests would say Mass. I saw that several people were sitting here and there in prayer or meditation.

In a glass box in a recessed area behind the altar lay the remains of my hero. Along with the others in my group, I joined the long queue of people waiting to pass by the saint.

Soon it would be my turn. My excitement built as the moment grew closer.

It was so wonderful to come face to face with the incorrupt body of Padre Pio. In that instant, my dreams were fulfilled. Inside, I felt a warm glow and my whole being felt serene and wrapped in a blanket of peace. I embraced these special moments in my heart and felt I could have stayed there forever in sacred silence because it was so wonderful, but of course, I knew he wasn't there just for me. So after a few moments, I slowly moved on and sat down on a bench nearby.

After some time sitting in prayer, my friends and I left the crypt. As we walked around, we visited some shops, and these ones were quiet and discreet compared to the ones we had seen on the streets. In a few of them, you could buy Mass cards for those living as well as dead, so I purchased a few.

In the company of my friends, we explored some more areas of the sanctuary before making our way back outside to the warm sunshine. I felt a sense of renewed awakening come over me, and awareness of the beauty of everything around me in a way I hadn't seen up to now. I also felt so grateful for being able to experience this wonderful place and silently thanked Father Kevin for his wise words that if I stepped back from all judgment, the sacred beauty of San Giovanni would be revealed. He was so right.

I felt I didn't want to leave this sacred space just yet so told my friends I would see them later, and went back to the main church again for a short while. As I sat in the large spacious interior, I reflected on how my spirit responded to certain locations and situations. I believe it learned to separate from my body during my brushes with death throughout my life, and that means it is a bit more ungrounded than other people's. Nowadays it becomes quite reactive around higher spiritual energies.

So then when my spirit feels spiritual realms are close, it wants to go home to them. It has been said that when people fall in spirit that they may be astral travelling. In this state, some spirits may go to trouble spots around the globe to help with healing. Additionally, they may also be whisked off to be trained by angels they have an affinity with. But from what I can fathom, all my own spirit seems to want to do is go home where it feels it belongs, to heaven.

Apparently, a lot of us astral travel while sleeping. Certainly, it would be wonderful if my falling in spirit only happened at night when I was at home in bed. Then it would not be so embarrassing and make a show of me in front of others. I am sorry to say that a few people see me as a drama queen and keep their distance from me when it happens. For me, it's like the body is suddenly switched off, and there is nobody home for a short period of time.

That led me to think of something else. There had been lots of good times and laughs throughout the journey so far, but because I was feeling detached a lot of the time, I missed out on participating in a good deal of the fun and the crack. I promised to myself that if I came on another pilgrimage I would ground myself more, so I could connect better with those around me and with the places I visited. That would be my plan, but I know I am not always in charge.

On this pilgrimage, I seemed to have more connection with the priests and religious of San Giovanni than I did with my fellow travellers. Part of it was because I was in my most favourite place in the world, and I wanted to know all about it—and the priests and nuns who were deeply connected to

San Giovanni were the ones who were most informative, and were only too willing to share their stories.

A special prayer I picked up in San Giovanni is one I say often now:

Help me, Father, to be present always. Because it's only when my body, soul and spirit are united.

And I am fully present to You and Your people That I can channel Your love and light to all I meet. In my quieter moments share them with me, Help me feel Your presence, Then allow me the honour of service.

Padre Pio is an amazing example of how we can create a better world by living a life both practically and spiritually. He certainly learned how to be present to people in the real world. I decided that when I got back home I would try not to run away when things became hard. Additionally, my vision of living in a place where healing people was always paramount was beginning to become clearer.

I said to God, 'I may never achieve the heights that Padre Pio reached, but I'll do my best to be of service to you and hold and honour the light you gave me. I am privileged by the gift of life you have bestowed on me, and the precious moments I have experienced. I don't feel worthy to be of service, and I feel humbled in your presence. I know there are many good people in the world whom I would see as more spiritual than me, so I am grateful you chose me to do your work on Earth and help people. I know there is always more to learn, and I will try to be a little more patient and wise as I move forward with you and the angels by my side.'

Chapter 18
Glove and Cross

Looking back, there were many highlights for me on this trip, and the fact that I was there at all was a wonderful gift and an incredible experience. It was my first time on a pilgrimage, but it won't be my last. The priests who led the pilgrimage and the countries and people we visited touched my heart and soul deeply. Already I was sure that my life would never be the same again, and I realised I was changing from the inside out.

So here I was, with my world constantly changing in a great way, and events around me opening me up to Spirit even more than had happened to me in Ireland. I had to just trust and allow things to happen, and at that point, I really began to believe my life was being divinely guided. While in San Giovanni, one of my favourite things to do was to get up early every morning before breakfast to go the Mass and hear the monks singing. Their voices were amazing.

I felt it was a real privilege to be in the presence of these holy men, singing their hearts out and raising the spirits of all those present. The atmosphere there was so peaceful and welcoming. Then, after Mass and breakfast, we would be informed as to what our schedule would be for that day.

One morning, we learned we would be visiting the Way of the Cross, an outdoor Stations of the Cross. Before we did, however, we had to stop off at a place nearby where we would each pick a small cross to carry with us while doing the stations. The cross was a reminder of how Christ carried his cross to death, and then to resurrection. I also felt it was a reminder of the way we should carry our burdens in life till we pass over when we will eventually find our own resurrection.

Other groups had arrived before us, so we had to wait our turn. While we stood there I observed the behaviour of a few women. It really is funny how people can get stressed about the little things in life. These particular ladies were having an argument about which cross they should take. I thought their row was absurd—to me, a cross was a cross was a cross.

I called out, 'Just pick one,' because I was aware there were a lot of people behind us wanting to come in and choose their crosses. Jesus must have been laughing looking down at this lot! The debate ended quickly when a priest entered the room. The "children" quickly calmed down, and without any further delay, they made their choices and emerged with a cross.

The Way of the Cross is situated near the old church of Santa Maria Dela Grazie. It begins via a huge wide staircase, and from there a forested pathway leads up a hill. Sixteen sculptures are positioned at regular intervals along the way; fourteen are of the Stations of the Cross, one is of Padre Pio, and standing at the top of the hill is a large statue of the risen Christ.

We all walked in contemplation, saying the Rosary together. Between the decades of the Rosary, one or other of the priests talked about the importance of prayer and of Padre Pio's life and journey. There was always something more to learn about this amazing man. We were told about his childhood, his parents, and the fact he was an ordinary person and could be grumpy sometimes.

Well, with everything he suffered in life, I could hardly blame him. It can't have been pleasant to have had holes in your hands and feet which bled for fifty years of your life. You might be entitled to get a bit frustrated now and again if you had endured what he had experienced.

With that thought in mind, I felt it kind of put things in perspective. We all can make a very big deal out of minor challenges and ailments at times, just like the ladies fighting over the crosses. The only way to really heal is to have a personal desire and motivation to be well and to take responsibility for ourselves.

For sure, no one escapes pain, hurt or trauma in life. It's not how we go down that matters. It's how we come back up. Our faith and hope can be challenged at times, but it is how we find our way back to our core that is the important thing.

When we do, we once again connect with God and find our faith and hope renewed and strengthened by the difficult events we faced.

During the following couple of days, we did the Way of the Cross again as well as going on a lot of walks up and down other hills and pathways, some of which were very rocky. But it was worth it to feel the serenity and peace all around and enjoy the scenery in this special place. After lunch, we would take our siestas, which took a while to get used to. I couldn't imagine siestas taking off in Kerry any time soon!

One afternoon, while fasting on my bed, I found myself daydreaming. I wondered if I could get a monk's habit like Padre Pio's. Yes, I know, those habits were made for men. But I chuckled as I thought of the people back in Ballybunion and what they would think if they saw pint-sized me walking the streets of Tralee in a monk's habit! They would probably say I'd lost the plot, but I'm not sure my Tony would be surprised. And I think my family would just accept it and say something like, 'Ah that's just Mary doing her thing.'

Actually, a few of my siblings might indeed see me as a little mad, but there was nothing unusual there. All in all, though, it would be fun to get a rise out of them. And some of them might even want to try on the habit! I smiled to myself, and in the warmth and peace of the gentle Italian day, I drifted into a relaxing sleep.

Then I had a dream, and in the dream, I was taking on the mantle of Padre Pio, along with his robes and sandals. When I awoke I thought, well that was curious! Later, I met one of my friends and shared my dream with her. I giggled a bit as I related it, to her because I just thought it was a bit strange.

But my friend invited me to see what the dream might have really been about. She interpreted it as the saint asking me to be of service and showing me that he would work through me and with me in helping others. Her words certainly gave me pause for thought.

I suppose if you look at the people organising the Padre Pio pilgrimages around the world, there is no doubt they have been called to service. The same goes for the teams organising the Padre Pio Masses and those who carry the saint's relics to different venues in different countries, bringing healing and love wherever they go. These good people are contributing to

Padre Pio's work, healing in his name and caring for others. So, even now, many years after his death, Padre Pio is still working for us, and I thought that in my small way, I too could help send the healing.

On another day, we were in the English Office again. Tea and biscuits were always on offer there, and what Irish person could refuse that? Well, funnily enough, I don't drink tea myself. I was thirsty, though, and asked a friend who was queuing up for the beverage to bring me back a glass of water. As we sipped our drinks, a monk spoke up and said he hoped we were enjoying our pilgrimage.

We all said yes we were, and I looked at him from the back of the room. I felt this particular person radiated quite an amazing calm serenity. He then went on to talk about the beautiful soul that was Padre Pio, and towards the end of his talk added that the saint would have really appreciated all of us pilgrims coming to San Giovanni. But he wouldn't want them to honour him—he'd want them to honour Christ and His Father.

Pio's humility was very important to him, and his devotion to Christ was very deep. This could be seen in the way he carried his stigmata and the pain he felt. Then the monk told us that if we wished, we could come up again, row by row, and receive a blessing with the cross and one of Padre Pio's gloves, which is one of his special relics. In his lifetime, the saint wore gloves every day to protect the wounds of his stigmata, and these gloves are now just one of the special gifts he left us all when he went home.

I could hardly believe it—I was to touch the cloth that touched the hands that had borne Christ's wounds. I could not imagine being closer to Pio or Christ right then. In great anticipation, I joined the queue, and then, when it was my turn for the blessing, all of a sudden my spirit said bye-bye, and I was gone. I learned later that one of my friends said, 'Don't touch her, it's Spirit doing that. Give her space.'

I came around a few minutes later sitting on the floor, wiping my eyes and feeling a bit dazed. One of the priests was beside me and said I was as pale as a ghost. I could see his concern and said, 'Don't worry, Father, it's OK. For me, it's normal, and I've got used to this.'

Then, as another priest came over I collapsed again. I was half in and out of consciousness this time, and as I was helped sit up on a chair, I heard the stone bells again, ringing softly in the background. Once more my spirit was gifted to hear that wonderful angelic music.

Eventually, I completely came to, none the worse for wear. The blessings resumed, and when they were over and people dispersed to go about their day my friends asked me if I wanted to join them on a wander around. I said thanks, but I wanted to visit the crypt again and would see them later.

The crypt was so peaceful and gentle. I have to say every time I went there it soothed my soul. Sitting on one of the benches, I thought about the experience I'd just had. I knew at times it could frighten people, and I wish it didn't. I wasn't sick or ill or anything.

Thankfully, I am aware now there are many people the world over who are also affected like this whenever they are in areas of high spiritual energy. That knowledge has actually helped me accept myself more. I'd love to know what my spirit is up to when it separates from my body, but I just have to try and understand that is just the way it is.

Another monk, an older man, who had seen my falling in spirit sought me out and gave me a gift bag of memorabilia from the shrine. He said, 'You are special. Continue whatever good work you are doing and don't be perturbed about what other people think. Just remember Pio is always with you and Archangel Michael is always protecting you.'

I was so grateful and honoured, and I thanked him for his very kind words.

As the pilgrimage came to a close, I felt sad that this wonderful experience was to end but also looked forward to what the future might bring. Looking up at the night sky on the last evening, I thought, my goodness… all over our world there are people watching the same night sky and the same sun. We are all really connected. We may live in Ireland, New York or Australia, but Mother Earth cares for each and every one of us wherever we are.

As we go around our daily lives, we are all just trying to survive. Sometimes we do it with energy, love and passion. Sometimes though, we find ourselves in a world of challenges, isolation and loneliness. Life can certainly be a rollercoaster at times so let's find compassion in our hearts for our fellow man and woman.

Being in Medjugorje and San Giovanni was living proof of the need for support and acknowledgement of that connection amongst us all. When I was told by the angels in the church in Lixnaw that I was going on this pilgrimage, I almost laughed. I thought it was impossible at that time in my life, yet here, I was at the end of a wonderful spiritual journey which had enriched my soul beyond measure. To know how it's OK to be me and to accept myself as I am is a very important lesson that has come from the pilgrimage. I also learned that we can't love others until we love ourselves. I understand now that I have to place all my faith and trust in God and not give up or stagnate ever again.

Far from the initial disappointment I felt when I first saw San Giovanni Rotondo and all the commercialism, after those few days there I was in a state of deep peace, celebrating the place and the people. Also, I realised that my conflicted emotions had a reason: they were to help me learn lessons and teach me that Spirit is everywhere and God is always at hand no matter where we are in the world.

Even as I left San Giovanni and Italy, I knew I'd return. You could count on it. I was aware my connection with it would last till the day I die and Padre Pio would be there as I pass into spirit. I also knew that he would never abandon me in my hour of need. There would be times I'd fall, and I would have challenges to overcome, but he would be there to pick me up when necessary and set me on the right path again.

It was a pleasant enough trip home to Dublin. The humour was good and people were happy, if tired. I think we all felt it was a privilege to have had the chance to be part of this trip and have our lives touched by precious moments and memories. As we said our final goodbyes to each other at Dublin Airport, there were hugs and kisses and a few tears. The amazing journey we all had experienced made it possible for people to forge real friendships within a relatively short space of time.

I had been away for only eight nights, but because I experienced so much while I was there I was exhausted by the time I got home and felt I needed a holiday! If I had been asked to stay in San Giovanni, either to wash the dishes at the hotel or wash the floors in the monastery, I would have been tempted to do so. To be in that atmosphere, to feel so close to Padre Pio and Spirit, I guess I could have called it a type of spiritual home for me.

Within a few days, it was almost like the pilgrimage had been like a lovely dream, as my ordinary life in Ireland resumed. However, I knew it would remain forever a special space of time that was given to me, which has eased my fears and confirmed my path. To all those who made the trip happen, I owe a debt of gratitude. I have to say the pilgrimage organisers did a great job because everything was so well-organised. The hotels we stayed in were lovely, the staff and people everywhere were warm and friendly, and the food throughout was wholesome and delicious.

For me, Padre Pio the saint became Padre Pio the human being on this trip, and it was great to see the many facets of his personality brought to life. I could see now he was someone you could talk to and who had great empathy for people. He showed me how human beings can do extraordinary things and how one individual can really make a difference. I believe I am now in a better place mentally and spiritually and am happy to use my gifts to serve God in whatever way He wants me to. I also know I need to trust my inner voice more and take more time to listen with an open heart to the voice of the Spirit.

I am grateful for all the blessings I received on the pilgrimage, and that I was so deeply touched by divine love and mercy. In my mind and my heart, I will forever treasure the memories of that wonderful trip. And all that is left to be said to the monks and priests and nuns over there is, Keep the kettle on, I'll be back, and soon!

Chapter 19
Living and Learning

It was great to be back home in Ballybunion. There is an old Irish saying, *Nil aon tinteân mar da thinteän, féin,* which means, 'There is no fireside like your own fireside. It was lovely to walk the beach again with my dog, Alex, and breathe in the fresh Kerry autumnal air, mingling with the scent of the sea. But even though I was at home and in familiar territory, I felt different. I was much more at peace within myself, probably more than I had ever been before in my life. I had discovered stillness and saw that maybe all the trauma in my life had a purpose and that my story was unfolding as it was meant to.'

As I resumed my normal life, my mind was still full of all the things that happened while I was on the pilgrimage. I spent a lot of time processing the learnings I experienced while at the same time trying to integrate my thoughts, feelings and desires about who I was and where I wanted to go next. I knew that wherever that would be, it would all be according to the divine plan, and I was willing to trust that. However, living that way didn't mean I wasn't curious about what was in store for me.

My mind would often wander back to special moments I had experienced on the pilgrimage, like when I heard the "The Bells of the Angelus" hymn from the stone bells of San Giovanni. Upon my return, some acquaintances told me, 'Catherine, you were always away with the fairies, but you're even worse now, you're barely here at times.' I didn't mind their comments too much: most of them came from people who had preconceived ideas and judgments about me that dated back a long time, and they didn't know the new happier, spiritually reawakened mc. And who were they to judge anyway? Before, I may have become a bit irked at their comments, but no one was going to disturb the peace and magic I now felt within myself.

One of my biggest lightbulb moments of the journey was that if ever there had been a doubt in my mind that I was created to help people and be of service, there wasn't any more.

Everything that happened and all that I experienced in Pio's country helped me see clearly that wherever my heart and spirit led, I would have to follow.

I knew that from this point onward I needed to get out of my own way and stop overthinking, You'd think this might be easy to do, but it's not. Control is something that is very hard to surrender. Trusting people, places and life was something I stopped doing a long time before because of all the problems I faced growing up and as an adult.

Trusting in the wrong people resulted in tremendous pain and suffering, so opening up to trust was something that for me carried a lot of fear. It was a testing time for the new me, but I did see that God had started to create a better support structure around me. My life was definitely improving, and if

I had the courage to stay open, I believed I would get a real chance to play my part and fulfil my life's purpose.

The pilgrimage and the Padre Pio Masses weren't the only places where I felt deep connections with the Spirit. Several years previously I had a few other experiences which showed God and the angels had not forgotten about me and were supporting me when I needed them most. I'd like to share with you one of those very special events, which was a real gift from Spirit at the time.

I had arranged to meet our accountant whose business was located on Dingle Road, and on that particular day, it was really stormy with pelting rain. As I drove along in my little car, I felt the weather outside matched how I felt inside. I was in considerable emotional pain at that moment in time and wasn't sure if I wanted to continue living. I was early for the appointment and decided to call into a nearby church to see if I could elicit some support for my tired soul.

Maybe I would light some candles and say a prayer. Despite everything in my life that had gone wrong I had not lost my faith or my love of God, and I always felt He loved me even if I didn't always feel I was heard by Him or that He gave me the help I needed. It was like the prospect of a lotto win: anytime soon would be good!

The church was warm and inviting, and that was probably more pronounced because of the driving rain and the howling wind outside. There were no lights on and everything was cast in a dim half-light. The church was empty but for me. As I made my way up the centre aisle, I could make out paintings of the Stations of the Cross on the walls on either side. Beside the altar at the top was a votive candle rack where some candles had already been lit, and the soft flickering glow from the flames gave the whole interior of the church a gentle, sacred atmosphere.

At the altar, I saw that the red light of the Tabernacle was on, letting all good Catholics know that Christ was present, as well as telling me I was not alone. As I stood there for a few moments, the sound of the entrance doors banging intruded on the stillness of the church as they kept opening and closing with the frequent gusts of wind.

I lit my candles, found a seat and sat down. Despite the noise of the doors, I was conscious of the space Spirit had gifted me and murmured a few prayers. I was jolted back to earth a few minutes later when out of the blue a young man came in. He was in his twenties and very handsome, with shoulder-length hair, a trench coat and tan shoes. He walked up to the candle rack and lit a few candles.

To my surprise, I could feel a gentle and peaceful energy emanating from him and radiating around the main body of the church. My worries and fears trickled away, and I was infused with a sense of calm, safety and well-being. The man came into the church and left it three times, but at no point did I feel stressed or threatened by his presence.

It just so happened that when I finally got up to leave I saw the man had turned around to walk out at the same time. As he passed me by, we made eye contact, and he smiled at me. He had beautiful sky-blue eyes that were full of compassion, and when he looked at me, it felt like he really knew me and understood me. I smiled back at him, and then he quietly walked out of the church and went back out into the storm. I was left standing mystified by what had transpired. I sat back in my seat and was overcome by a sense of knowing that everything would be all right.

After a little while, I looked at my watch and, realising it was nearly time for my appointment, rose and walked to the door. I tamed the handle and pushed. No leek So then I pulled. Again no luck. These were the doors that had been banging open and closed all the time I'd been there. What was going on?

I tried a few more times to no avail. I was actually locked in. The doors were, in fact, locked so solidly it was as if they were glued, nailed and bolted to the frame. But how was that possible? Did the young man lock me in? No. I just somehow knew he would not have done that.

Then, out of the corner of my eye, my attention was drawn to a small piece of paper fluttering on top of a small wooden table near the door. I was baffled. I was sure there had been no table or paper when I came into the church. It was like they had just appeared out of nowhere. Not only that, a little bottle of holy water sat beside the paper.

I went over and picked up the paper, and on it, I saw a prayer to Archangel Michael. As I lifted up the bottle with my other hand, suddenly the doors blew open again, and I intuitively knew that I had found what I was meant to find, and was now free to go. I realised I would be late for my accountant if I did not hurry, so I ran out the door, got into my car and set off down the road.

I arrived at the accountant's place of business just on time, when I greeted him, I moaned about the horrible stormy weather.

He just laughed and said, 'Catherine, we've been having the most beautiful day all day.'

I looked out the window, and to my amazement, I saw it was a lovely sunny day, with not a cloud in sight.

'Did you take a nap in your car before you came here?' he joked. 'Maybe you were dreaming.'

But no, I wasn't, for I knew that on the seat of my car, outside there was a bottle of holy water and a piece of paper with a prayer on it. As Yeats put it in "The Ballad of Father Gilligan", 'He sent one of His great angels down to help me in my need.'

When I told the accountant I had visited the church down the road, he laughed again and said, 'Ah. You hear a lot of stories about that place.'

That was enough to confirm for me that the church held a special sacred essence and that what I had experienced was absolutely real. We then proceeded with our business, and later on the drive home, I reflected on the incident. Everything in me told me that the beautiful young man who had appeared in the church was Archangel Michael, and he was affirming I was protected. This angel is more often pictured as a fearsome warrior rather than a preppy young man, but there you go. The form he took actually made me feel secure, safe and grounded. It was a very gentle and benign energy.

Life is full of spiritual mysteries if you are just open to them. I have learned along the way that when Spirit connects with you, you don't feel afraid at all. They help to support and protect you and hold you in love. Sitting in the church with the young man, aka Archangel Michael, was like getting a warm hug. It was exactly what I needed at the time, and I was so grateful for it, as it helped to see me through the storm.

A while after that I went with a friend to visit Archangel Michael's Well in Lixnaw. As I walked into the space, I could not come close to expressing the tranquillity I felt. That started a love affair with the well that has continued to this day. I would invite everyone to visit this lovely place and experience the gentle energy for themselves. For me, it was a reminder that in this crazy world, we can feel at peace in the gentle sacredness of such locations.

It was a few years later that I went to the Padre Pio Mass in Lixnaw where I experienced the first of many fallings in spirit. In more recent times, if I was ever visiting Lixnaw I would visit both the church and Archangel Michael's Well. It was incredible and amazing—the peace of the well was greatly mirrored in the peace of the church. I would just sit in the stillness of both places and soak in the peace. They were so close together in one little village, and it just shows you can find spirituality everywhere.

So now, after years of neglect, pain, abuse and abandonment, I felt the Spirit reaching out and touching my heart in a most profound way. But just as important was the process of educating myself more about Spirit. The journey of the physical body on Earth may have a start and a finish, but the spiritual journey is eternal. I knew that at some stage, Saint Michael the Archangel, Padre Pio and I would work together. I didn't know how, but I knew one day we would get there.

When I visited the different sacred sites, as well as hearing heavenly music and smelling the presence of flowers and incense which is not in our everyday reality, sometimes I also daft a, touch of a hand, or a warm gentle brush of a breeze on my hair or face. One way or another, Spirit let me know that they were present. It was a great feeling, and it made me smile every time it happened. It was like a reminder, lest I'd ever forget, that they were watching over me and helping me do God's work.

I knew that Spirit wanted me to be open and gain more and more spiritual knowledge. This was shown to me in different ways. For example, on occasions, I'd feel the playful pulling of my ears by the angels.

When I was going to hear good news my right ear would get pulled gently and when the same happened to my left ear, it meant something not so good was on the horizon. It was all a learning curve. Sometimes nothing happened for ages and then all of a sudden, a splurge of little events would let me know they hadn't gone away. And then there would be another gap for a while. It seemed to be the way Spirit worked.

I used to feel guilty because I'd sometimes eat the wrong food or didn't get enough exercise, and there was Spirit always looking over me and taking care of me. To be honest, I have always been a bit of a brat, rarely doing what I'm told. I have been doing things wrong for as long as I can remember and much as I regret saying it, I reckon I'll misbehave till the day I die. Maybe it's just the human condition, but just like I can't give up on my human frailties, I know the Spirit will never give up on me because they said they never would, and I believe in them, love them and trust them.

On one occasion, I was in hospital. I'd had a procedure, and I was waiting for Tony to collect me. I found out he was going to be a bit delayed so decided to mosey around the little hospital bookshop. I love books, so it was a pleasure to browse some of the shelves and flip through a few titles. I was happy to find a book that interested me, so I took it up to the cashier.

As I looked away momentarily from the woman behind the counter, out of the blue—I have absolutely no idea how—

two packets of angel cards fell into my hands. The girl at the cash desk looked at me a little surprised.

I think the angel would like me to buy these, I laughed.

'It certainly looks that way,' she replied with a smile.

It was clear those cards were coming home with me. They had obviously decided that I needed to learn about them. It was weird as I would never have looked at these kinds of cards before. I had always been a bit wary of New Age stuff, having come from a very traditional conservative Catholic family. But here I was, being introduced by Spirit to my first angel cards. At the time, I wasn't sure why I had them but knew I would find out at some stage.

As time went on, it became clear a new awareness was entering my life. You could call it an expansion of consciousness. I had been used to priests guiding me on my spiritual journey, not angels, saints and spirits. It's funny, looking back I can see they were always pointing me in the right direction and pushing me forward at a pace I could live with and learn from. Now I understand divine timing is clearly linked to the understanding that when the student is ready, the teacher appears.

Many years ago I worked in the Castle Green Hotel in Ballybunion. Like many other businesses, it is now closed and has passed into history. In the hotel, there was a staff member called Moss Pendy, a spiritually gifted man who was now sitting with the angels. On our breaks, we used to chat a lot. Well, he did most of the talking, which knowing me is unusual enough because I do like to talk! But the things he spoke about were so interesting, and I just loved listening to him.

I now know he was sensitive and very intuitive, but at the time, I never dreamed he could have been a teacher sent my way. In those days, I didn't see myself as intuitive and was just intrigued by the things this good soul said. Along the way, I shared with him that my family had, for many generations, been blessed with gifts of spiritual awareness, precognition and healing. I also talked to him about my lovely Uncle Willie and the hidden secrets he never got to tell me. Moss promised that gradually over time I'd see the secrets being revealed. He also said that as I learned more about myself, I would open up more to the person I was meant to be.

Moss told me a lot of things that did not make any sense to me back then, but now do. He recognised my connection to spirit, my ability to work in healing and my ability as a seer. At the time, I politely declined to see those things in myself. There is no doubt we can be blind to what is right in front of our noses! Moss was also precognitive and told me once that four people would die in the dining room of the hotel and a resident musician would die by the end of the season.

It was not a nice thing to hear but the strange thing is, all these deaths happened just as he said they would. He also told me I would have a car accident, which did happen, and informed me of a few other events in my life that would take place in the future—and they all eventually unfolded just as he had predicted.

Eventually, I moved on from that job and lost touch with this good man. All the things he foretold about my future career were right, and wherever he is, I want to thank him so much for the gift of his great wisdom and friendship.

Chapter 20
Awakening to My Purpose

Sleeping Beauty is a wonderful tale, full of magic, fairy dust and make-believe. Well, I believe there is a bit of Sleeping Beauty in all of us. When we become more self-aware and look deep within, we realise there is so much more to discover. I used to think I knew who I was, but over time, I realised that I believed other people's perceptions about me and who I was more than I did myself. I have had to do a lot of self-reflection and healing over the years to let go of all the old judgements and criticisms in order to find the real me.

As a result, my inner beauty gradually awakened, and I slowly moved towards the person I was meant to be, freeing my heart a little bit at a time, and working for my heroes, Archangel Michael, Padre Pio and Our Lady. They have all been there with me through challenging times, including the horror and trauma associated with the difficult births of my children.

Believe me, I could be grumpy and went through lots of periods where I wanted to stay as I was. There is no doubt it is easier to hold onto the conditioning of the past and behave out of it rather than take responsible ownership of the self to create a new future. It is amazing how fear can keep you trapped. Going through all the skeletons in my closet was not something I was prepared for or even particularly interested in doing up to then, but my angels knew what was best for me, and they set about sending people into my life who would help me open up. I had to start seeing and understanding where my judgments about myself came from and to realise that often people were wrong in their judgements of me.

Personal responsibility is important in the spirit world and the angels want to see us grow into who we are created to be and do the work we are meant to do while on Earth. We need to be mindful that even though they can guide us and be there for us, we need to solve our own problems and take an active part in healing ourselves. I sometimes wondered if I was too much for the poor angels as I had a lot of anger in me. But in truth, I knew the angels were always supporting me, no matter what. I saw over time that the more I took account of my feelings in a positive way the less I felt controlled by others. As a consequence of this change, I felt more secure and confident in myself.

It is fascinating really that God chose me for this work. I am certainly no angel and have many flaws. There is no one out there who needs to tell me how human I am. Yet here He was inviting me to heal my wounds and understand my path. I know that if I had less anger I would have moved forward faster, but that was just the way it was.

I could only learn and grow at my own pace. It seemed that as far as my spiritual helpers were concerned, it was about patience and self-control so that the learning was thorough and complete. The angels showed me so much love and compassion, but I am sure they were probably irritated with me at times too!

The outward journey of my life included the horror story of my childhood up to the visit of Archangel Michael in the church on the Dingle Road. As I reviewed my past through different eyes, I discovered to my relief that many of the things I thought were my fault, weren't. I also found out that being labelled as not good enough from the beginning by the people around me had a profound effect on my self-esteem. Now I see that unfortunately, I believed what they said.

It took a surprisingly long time to unlearn these beliefs and realise my true worth. When I was still unsure of my own value, the slightest praise or compliment given to me nearly had roe winning for the hills in fear and embarrassment. I'd often feel like telling that person, 'Don't be silly, there is nothing special about me.'

At this stage in my life, I was sure I knew everything there was to know about myself. I was a Ballybunion housewife with two children and a good husband who was doing his best to make ends meet. I had two lovely dogs and had accepted I was going to grow old gracefully, just as my parents were doing and their parents had done before them. I was content in my own home, on my own land. I knew I still had some skeletons rattling around in my closet, but if I didn't hear or see them and if I ignored them, I could pretend they had no effect on me. I could just soldier on in my life regardless of the pain I carried, with a smile on my face and a sparkle in my eyes.

The collection of events which had happened to me in more recent times definitely changed my view on life. The more I got rid of my skeletons the more my intuitive gifts developed. I learned that this was because my third eye was opening up, and I was setting my spirit free. Now this was not something I could see in the mirror! No, this was an invisible essence guiding me into a new way of thinking about God and spirituality. As much as introspection could make me feel uncomfortable at times, it also made me curious, and I wanted to know more.

This extra knowledge of myself gave me a different impression of the Father, Spirit and the angels than I'd ever had before. A real connection with them was now possible, and I understood they were meant to be an active part of my life. All I had to do was learn to listen and get out of my own way. They would help me do the rest.

Sometimes I found it hard to believe that God, Archangel Michael, the Virgin Mother and Padre Pio were calling me into service. After what I had experienced up to date, I actually sometimes thought Spirit was just having a laugh at my expense. But they weren't, you know. They were giving me hope and demonstrating what real faith and trust looked like.

Spirit tried lots of things to help me move forward, and I can see there was order in what they did. When they showed me something spiritual and sacred about myself I moved towards the gifts they were shedding light on. And then when they seemed absent, I'd step back into my old fears and hide and become almost invisible again. But bit by bit I was making progress.

After the events that happened in Lixnaw along with the visit of Archangel Michael in the church and the surprising gift of the angel cards, it was clear something special was happening. I have to say I was intrigued and started to look around me with more awareness for more signs of Spirit in my life. When I did, different people, places and events came into my life to continue and build the process of my awakening and take me into a deeper level of awareness. The more I looked, the more I found, and I can see now how I was used at times, even unknown to myself, to help other people develop and open up spiritually and also how they were used as a catalyst for spiritual change in my life. It was like 'The Buddha in me meets the Buddha in you for our mutual enlightenment.'

It became clear we are always teaching each other, even if sometimes we are unaware of the lessons being taught. I thought back to the young man who tried to poison me and how that event affected different people in different ways. It reflected my vulnerability and the darkness within the bad son. It taught his parents how they could, under certain circumstances, go against their own principles when it suited them. It taught the doctor who prayed for my life how caring and compassionate he was and, lastly, the priest who came to pray for me demonstrated his strong faith when he said, 'She'll be fine. She has work to do.'

Now, I can see that in many ways, my journey to enlightenment, which continues to this day, was not necessarily always in a straight line. However, I was where I was meant to be at each stage of my journey. It was a process that slowly unfolded, like peeling an onion one layer at a time. As a child, I had shielded myself with protective layers, but in so doing moved away from the essence of who I was. Then, the older I became, I moved further away from my true self. Now, as each one of those layers came off, I gained precious learnings and became closer to my own divine truth.

I also realised that as a child, I had no problem being on my own but also liked the company of those who were dear to me. However, as negative things happened to me I retreated more and more into myself, and eventually, I was left quite isolated. On my own, and in my own world, I felt safe and played with the little fairies under the bridge at home for hours.

Looking back now, I feel so blessed that these elementals honoured me with their presence as they definitely helped me retain some of my magic. I have a sense they knew they could accept and trust me and that I in return could be a friend to them. Furthermore, my love for nature and the animals on our little farm greatly supported me in the midst of troubled times, and I am so grateful for the amazing experiences I had back then that gave me some joy and happiness in my childhood.

People were not ready to welcome my uniqueness when I was younger, but I am glad to see the world now seems to be more accepting of children who are born with special gifts, and who can see and hear the Spirit. In gaining greater clarity and understanding as an adult, I can now reclaim my own little child, accept myself more and move ahead in life, safe in the knowledge that I may be a bit different. I am not strange or odd, I am just the way God created me.

One day a young woman came to me and thanked me for what I did for her mum. Her kind words came at a time when I could have done with a boost. A short time beforehand I had been in the local hospital and spent some time with this girl's mother, a lovely woman who had cancer and was dying. We talked for a while, and I gave her a medal from Medjugorje.

I told her I would say a prayer for her at Archangel Michael's Well, and when I did that I asked God to give the lady a gentle passing. Later, the daughter told me her mum passed peacefully and said she was very grateful for my help.

To be honest, all I did was pray for her. When she passed, Earth lost a beautiful soul and heaven gained an angel.

Over the next period of time, I somehow found myself attracting people towards me who would tell me their life stories. This was something that had never happened to me before and was a bit odd at first. Complete strangers, out of the blue, would come up to me wherever I was and talk to me about their difficulties in life. It wasn't long before I realised that this was no coincidence, and it was the other side giving these people a tender ear to unburden themselves to. I started to carry medals of Padre Pio and Our Lady with me to give to those who talked to me, and I prayed with them, asking for healing for them.

This all happened without any effort at all on my part, and I became aware that I was growing more nurturing, almost motherly. I also found I was also becoming a kind of confessor and counsellor as well. The more I surrendered to it, the more natural and normal it became.

I thank those people, as they mirrored back to me a value I'd never seen in myself, I began to see the real kindness and gentleness in my being, and how people responded to someone who was compassionate and listened to them. Gradually, I started to love myself more consciously and at a deeper level. Then, with that, the anger at all the hurts I was carrying did not seem so bad anymore. Those things drifted into the background and grew less important as I could see the strength of the light coming into my life, getting brighter day by day. It was a good feeling, and I gradually opened up to the realisation that I really could help people and make a difference in their lives.

By this time, I was getting to know my angel cards and was developing a real connection with them. They were beautifully illustrated with gentle messages of divine support, love, guidance and encouragement. In an indefinable way, they also carried a challenge for me to honour the light within me and others and to trust and believe. All was meant to be as it was at that moment. Every day, I would pick a card, and without fail, something would happen that would match the message that would have been on that particular card. It was amazing how they aligned – synchronicity at its best.

In the face of the traumas, I experienced in my earlier life it hadn't always been easy to see virtues in other people around me or in myself. However, now, as I was shedding my pain and hurt, I felt increasingly aware that we are all supported by the Spirit as we journey through life. My spiritual awakening was a call to love, honour and believe in a divine plan, and to reach beyond my fears, knowing our Father in heaven loves us all dearly. I also knew that I was being asked to consciously live my new spirituality—not to just hear it and speak it but to live it. For me, it was a real call to action.

Chapter 21
New Encounters

Down the years I have been asked, who answered for what was done to me and my babies? Who answered for the crimes against my family? Who answered for the poisoning of a young teenager who almost lost her life? No one.

Today, when I see people standing up for themselves when hospitals or other institutions let them down, I have mixed feelings. I am proud of those individuals for not allowing injustices to pass and for forcing those responsible to take account for their wrongdoings, but I am also angry with myself for not having protected myself better back then and not meeting certain issues head-on.

Sometimes I have to content myself by saying society was different back then, I lived in a generation where you were brought up not to rock the boat—more or less to avoid challenging those in authority. Instead of standing up for myself I allowed pain, hurt and injustice to fester and eat away at my soul. To this day, I can still feel the absolute injustice of it all, and how I acquiesced and lived as a victim for so many years. Maybe in some small way, if I had received justice, some more lives would have been saved.

The powerful voice of the new generation has been built on the unacceptable pain of previous generations. We owe a debt of gratitude to these people who have had the courage to speak out and not allow history to control them. Society now demands accountability and higher standards in all sectors of the community.

In telling my story now, I have achieved a level of peace and a greater understanding of my past, and have given little Michael and Lizzie a voice. Furthermore, because of all the growth and loaning I have experienced over the years if anything happens where I feel remotely wronged today, I can go to great extremes in my quest for justice. I am determined never to be taken advantage of again.

I am acutely aware now that in giving too much power to those in authority, we sometimes abdicate our own responsibility to ourselves and our neighbours. It does not make it any easier to stomach the fact that sometimes we were actually complicit in the cause of our own anguish. For a period of time, I did a great job of burying the pain deep inside my subconscious, pretending I was OK and trying not to think about it. Outwardly, however, you could see the angry me rise uncontrollably now and again.

I have to say I felt very vulnerable when I first went to therapy and the person working with me said I was a warm, sensitive and loving human being. I remember grumbling that they didn't know who I really was, but inside I felt so exposed, really exposed. How did the therapist know I was soft? Were my defences weakening? I clammed up straight away and rushed to rebuild the walls I needed to protect myself. Regardless of how negative these walls were they still kept me, in my eyes, safe. It was better that I ran further into myself and hid than lose yet another battle.

However, the time had now come when God and His angels were not about to let me hide anymore, so running was not an option. They were not going to allow me to believe my mask was who I was and were determined to expose the real me. In this crazy merry-go-round of putting up defences and having them stripped away, I slowly began to be able to love myself more, acknowledging I had a kind heart and caring soul and that I had a good sense of humour.

As I continued my personal healing journey, I met a fantastic person, Daniel, in an angel shop in Limerick. He was a psychic and soul reader and held group and individual sessions. I booked a reading with him, and I have to say his soft, gentle energy really appealed to me. He was such a beautiful soul, and we connected right away. Daniel was the type of person I was now drawing into my life—someone who was spiritual, uplifting and happy to support me.

When we sat down for my soul reading, I gave him my maiden name Catherine Brenda Mary Madigan. The information I got consisted of a map of my real journey on Earth, and he told me he got his messages from the angels. Before I met him, I'd had a dream of a Star of David and a number of symbols I'd never seen before. When he started talking about the same signs and symbols I had seen in my dream I could hardly believe it, but to be honest, by that point, I was getting used to "coincidences" and strange things happening around me. I told him about my dream, and he just smiled, proceeding to translate the symbols and their meanings.

They were messages for me that confirmed I was a spiritual medium and healer working out of knowledge and wisdom from many past lives, and that I had to trust the process I was currently experiencing. Daniel said my spiritual goals included learning to be more open-minded, tolerant, compassionate and understanding. It was part of my soul's mission on Earth, and I had to learn how to integrate those values into my life even in the face of many challenges along the way. I also had to realise I was a free spirit and would always resist being controlled, something I can see to this day.

He told me I should not keep myself imprisoned behind walls of my own making, or believe the conditioned thinking society imposed on me. To help me evolve in life, I should try and understand other people more, and not rush to judge them without thinking things through. For sure, I used to be a bit impetuous and react to situations instead of acting, so he was completely right about that! Another thing he said I had to do was lose my self-doubt and realise the true value of who I was. I also needed to learn to be patient and trust I would be supported at all times by those in the spiritual realms.

It was an important reading for me at the time, because it gave me real confirmation I was on the right path. I was so happy to meet someone so special and deeply spiritual, and am glad to say we are still great friends, many years later. I agreed with Daniel's assertion that even if this world is tough and things do go wrong, there is a purpose to it all. There is a plan and each of us has a part to play in it.

A new world was opening up for me before my very eyes, a world with opportunity. I was not sure where it was going to lead me, but I knew that someday, somehow, I would get there.

Around the same time, I met another person who was to help me along the way, a spiritual healer called Michael, who was also a medium and who held regular healing circles in North Kerry, not far from where I lived. I went to this man for reading along with a lady I knew called Breda, whom he used to work with. My reading was quite beautiful, and in it, Catherine, the nun whom I was called after, came through from spirit. Michael told me she gave me a gentle smile and an approving nod.

During the reading, we talked a lot about spiritual matters. It was great to be in Michael's company and hear about his experiences which involved regular visions from the spirit world. After the reading, I managed to get a photograph of Sister Catherine from another nun, Sister Mary Margaret, who was in the same order as Catherine, and she looked exactly as Michael had described her.

A little while after my reading I went along to one of Michael's group healing circles. These consisted of small groups of like-minded individuals who were keen to develop and further awaken their spirituality. They meditated and did readings and any issues which concerned them were shared with the group.

One of the things Michael did the first evening I went was to give those participating blank envelopes in which there were three different numbers. Depending on what each person received Michael would give him or her an appropriate reading. I got the numbers 1, 3 and 4. Apparently, number 1 was about my physical rescue and becoming more grounded. It was also an invitation to come out from behind my self-imposed prison to freedom and to make absolutely sure and certain no one would be able to put me in this prison again.

Number 3 was about my boundaries and the need to keep a safe space around myself. It also involved my need to be heard, the courage to speak my own truth, and the ability to find my own voice. Finally, Number 4 was about the intellect and how I needed to get out of my head and search for wisdom inside myself. I was to trust the wisdom that God had given me and realise that I had a valuable contribution to make on this Earth. With the information, I was given by Michael my mind started to open up to a very different way of thinking.

Soon after that, I went to Michael for one-to-one healing sessions, and during the healings, I received a lot of pictures in my mind of scenes from the Bible and the Rosary. These images included the Annunciation, Christ's baptism in the Jordan, the institution of the first Eucharist at the Last Supper, the Agony in the Garden, the Resurrection, and the Crowning of Our Blessed Lady, Mother of Perpetual Help. It was like all these images were on a cinema screen in my mind, and it was as if I was really recognising them for the first time. In the sessions, I also frequently saw images of several of the archangels. I couldn't recognise which ones they were but just knew they were archangels.

After attending the circle a number of times, Michael invited me to work with him and the group. The first night I went, I was a bit nervous. I was just beginning to gain confidence as a reader and could sense things now in a way I could only dream about at one stage. However, another woman who attended that evening did not like a message I received and gave to her and was angry with me.

I know now that some people go to mediums looking for particular information they long to hear, and if they get a message, they don't like they can project anger onto the messenger—and I was the messenger that evening. I felt like running away, but my friend Breda, who was also there that evening, told rue not to and said I should not let people bully me out of the work I was meant to do.

I realise now that sometimes people are not ready to hear what you have to say, even if it is the truth. In time, though, they may come to accept and understand the spiritual messages that were given to them. I have to remember that all is in divine timing.

On the way home after that event, Breda advised me to ring Michael. I did the next day, and we discussed the issue at length. Eventually, the week passed, and it was time for the next healing circle. This time, I saw that Michael had changed the format. Instead of placing numbers in blank envelopes, he placed flowers in them and then interpreted what they meant to whoever picked a particular envelope. The night was lovely, and the woman who had been angry with me actually acknowledged she had been in a bad place the previous week, and there had been truth in the message I gave her.

In this world, we are really learning all the time from both positive and negative things. If I hadn't been resilient, if I hadn't gone back to that healing circle I would never have received that resolution and confirmation of my message from that lady. In this way, I learned that the more I persevered the more I grew.

At Breda's home, a couple of weeks later, a few of us did an exercise that was similar to the one we did with Michael. We put different flower petals in separate envelopes, and then we each picked an envelope without looking at it. The one I got had a rose petal inside it, and I knew that represented the

Sacred Heart and sacrificial love. I still have that petal to this day.

I continued to work with Michael for a period of time and when I look back it is clear he brought structure, form and focus to my journey. I will be forever grateful for the roles he and Daniel played in supporting me on my path.

I continued to frequently visit the holy well and the church in Lixnaw, as well as working with priests and religious brothers and sisters. I seemed to find and attract into my life people on a similar Christian path and with a devotion to angels. If ever I encountered difficulties which challenged my new perspective on life, I knew they were there to provide me with further opportunities to grow.

I had gone to a number of angel and psychic readers by now and was constantly getting the same messages, that I was to help and support people as they tried to deal with challenges and difficulties on their journeys. I gradually came to realise that the more I helped others, the more enriched and fulfilled I felt in my own life. As I became happier and more joyful, I felt God's light becoming stronger and shining more clearly through me.

Chapter 22
The Door Is Finally Open

As we come to the end of the book, I'd like to talk about a few matters which are close to my heart. Hopefully, they will also provide you with a few insights and encouragement along the way on your own unique journey.

There were times when I felt like giving up on life, but Spirit forced me to stay because they told me I had work to do. I was told, *Fight, don't give up.* And I hung on in there, despite going through some tremendously difficult periods. In very different ways, my son and daughter also went through difficult times, and guess what? We are all still here today, and I hope we will have many bright days ahead of us as we continue to write the story of our lives.

Now, I understand the importance of living moment to moment, Life is constant change, and it doesn't rain all the time, nor is every day sunny. kike Irish weather, it's always changeable with plenty of rainbows.

In the work I do now, I have had a constant stream of people come to me who have lost someone they loved through suicide. It doesn't matter who you are, where you come from or what age you are—suicide can happen to anyone. We are all susceptible to the trials and tribulations of life. I am sure everyone knows someone who has been touched by suicide, whether it is a loved one, friend or associate.

There is no doubt it is a terrible shock to those left behind, but the person who died would not have wanted to distress anyone. They just wanted unbearable pain or mental anguish to stop, and maybe just couldn't see that the sun would rise again, and one day they would laugh and sing and dance again.

Something I have found along the way is that if some people want to end their lives here and cross over, it is often just not possible for them to succeed. God has to be ready to take you home, and if it is not your time, you won't go. Many people have tried suicide and failed, only to discover that there actually is light at the end of the tunnel, and life is worth living after all. Then again, some others have tried and have died. However, we should not judge anyone—we should show compassion and love to all and be aware that those who have passed are safe in the hands of the Father.

I believe very strongly the only way we can reduce the amount of people going home by suicide is to constantly work to make this world a better place. Each one of us could make a difference by living positively and being who we really are. We cannot and should not despair. We may not comprehend why certain things happen, but I am sure that there is a divine plan for everyone, and everything happens for a reason. We have to trust the process of living and dying, which can be hard because it is only in hindsight that we understand the meanings and learnings behind the challenges we face.

Maybe my own near-death experiences were to teach me to appreciate life more than I did, who knows? Looking back, I see I could have lived with more freedom and passion, joy and happiness. Nowadays, I am determined to live the gift of life with more confidence and courage. For a while in my life, all I saw was pain in the world, and it blinded me to all the goodness and all the joy. I am kinder to myself now and more patient and understanding of the phrase, "Sufficient unto the day", and hopefully, this gives me a better balance of work, rest and play.

There are times we might want to abdicate from our responsibility to help others and improve the community we live in. By believing all the evils everywhere are external forces that are beyond our reach and that we can do nothing about them, we can allow ourselves to wallow in despair. We should be constantly self-aware and learn how our behaviour can positively—or negatively—affect others. If we are bothered about something in our community or country, we can at least raise our voice or express an opinion. If we feel strongly about an injustice, then we need to put our shoulders to the wheel and change it. We need to learn that what we say and do matters.

We are far more powerful than we think, and it really is amazing how even one person can make a difference. Something as simple as a smile or a hug can be like a shiny pebble of positivity dropped into the murky waters of sadness. I believe that shining our light onto darkness substantially reduces evil, pain and hurt in this world and can have a ripple effect on the wider community. Perhaps we feel we are not important enough, but we are, and all change starts with us.

I believe that if we improve one small thing about our lives each and every day, we will create a much better world for ourselves and others. None of us has to climb Everest alone—we can do it together as a team.

The world is so full of prejudice, bigotry and strife, and we need to recognise we are all equal, regardless of race, colour or creed. I remember being horrified when I saw a video a while ago of an African-American mother who found her little child in floods of tears while scrubbing her soft little face. When the mother asked her what she was doing, she said she was trying to wash away the dirt. She wanted to be white. She wanted to be "clean".

Then there was another young girl who was overweight and cruelly teased by her peers. She stopped eating until finally near death she had a complete change of perspective and realised she didn't need to starve herself to be accepted. In fact, she needed no one to accept her except herself. Thank God she found that out before it was too late. With the help of doctors and therapy, she recovered, and years later, this beautiful lady became a star. Divinity is within us all.

We really need to be acutely aware of how much we all matter, and that each of us has an important contribution to make in the world. Negative thinking and behaviour often start in childhood and can go on to adversely affect us as adults throughout our lives. On the other hand, happiness and joy can be infectious and can make people feel really good about themselves as one person's warmth spreads to another.

Think for a moment of a home where fear and pain rule. What type of world would that create for any child? Now think of a home which is a place of love and equality, a haven of inclusion and acceptance regardless of who you are. Think of the child that comes from that environment, and now multiply that by every person on the planet, and just think what a wonderful world it would be.

Let us all shine our light on the shadow side of our being and heal it, so we can be the best of who we are. Sharing our light is a gift to everyone we meet, and by living consciously, we can change the world.

I believe that as long as we continue to develop weapons to use in war, then we are guaranteed there will be a day we will use them on the battlefield and people will die. I also think that if nations agreed tomorrow not to make any more weapons, with the way we are at the moment I'm sure we would find other ways of killing or fighting among ourselves. We must learn to live in more peaceful ways; otherwise, our children are destined to repeat the same mistakes.

Ironically, through conflict and pain many scientific and medical advances have been made, but what if we sowed the seeds of respect, admiration and achievement from all peoples everywhere and then development could happen through cooperation, altruism and love?

Imagine the difference that could be made to the world if enough money and resources were brought to global problems like poverty, famine, climate change, lack of education and other opportunities. We can but hope this will happen. Governments around the world may be saying they are trying their best to change the world but sometimes it seems like it is one step forward and two steps back, and the level of effort very much depends on what is going on at the time.

In Ireland, we are lucky to live in a relatively peaceful place, and the economy is fairly stable even though many challenges still need addressing like homelessness, domestic violence, the housing crisis and healthcare problems. I am glad I never tried to become a politician. You really have to know how to balance and juggle many issues to have a decent chance at sensible progress, equality and growth.

For those who really care, all the competing self-interests must be very frustrating. I know some of our politicians make mistakes, but these public officials need our support, not our criticism. Some of them are out for their own ends and egos, but not all of them are. I, for one, have to believe that there are some politicians with real integrity who do try and fight for their community.

I know there are no easy answers and feel the best I can do from where I stand is vote for the TDs whom I think have the best interests of the community at heart and those who will shape laws and policies which will help as many people as possible. I have a personal interest in health matters, and if I was working for the government, I would probably highlight this area to the exclusion of others! Age demographics are changing and people are living longer which means there is a great need for extra beds and services in hospitals. The follow-on from this is that more and more doctors and nurses are needed than ever before. Our medical personnel even now are understaffed and overworked. In saying this, I do understand that the public purse is limited and politicians can't be all things to all people, but we must find a better way than we have at the moment.

I remember watching an interview some years ago which featured an old politician who came from around the County Cavan area. He was retired and talking about the state of the country when he was an elected official. Cavan was affectionately known at the time as the pothole capital of Ireland. He said that the government back then had no money to fill in the potholes, and so they asked farmers to fill the holes themselves.

The farmers agreed and went and did their best to repair their roads, willing to go out on a limb to take responsibility for mending and improve the roads in their communities for the benefit of all. It's a good mindset—that we are all in this together. What a wonderful thing it is to go beyond our own needs at times and reach out to others who need assistance, both in our own country and across the globe.

Generosity lifts our spirits and creates a better world.

I am aware that many people and organisations are trying to make the world a better place, for example, the police, the army, non-governmental organisations like Amnesty International, the Red Cross, charities, and those in medical professions. There is also an army of community activists who silently go about making our lives better but often go unnoticed and unrecognised for their efforts. All of these groups would be sorely missed if they were not there.

With the help of many good people and Spirit, I am so much more content in my life now and have healed a lot of the trauma of my past. The person who poisoned me may have poisoned my body, but I will not allow him to damage my soul, spirit or mind. He does not define me any more—no one does. I am my own person. Similarly, I will not allow the hospital system which caused me so much pain to rob me of my belief in the great doctors and nurses who fought to save my babies and who went way beyond the call of duty to help me. I will not let myself be a victim of darkness anymore, and if I stumble and fall, I know I will rise again.

Understanding the pain I endured and integrating all the learning I received along the way will not diminish what I have been through, but it has made it easier to bear. It also helped me to reduce the impact of my pain and has enabled me to release a lot of anger and bitterness as I progress through life. I realise that I am both a teacher and a student and hope that I will give the best of myself to those around me in the future.

Once I used to criticise others, so I would not feel bad about myself. I no longer need to do this as I realise that to err is human, to forgive is divine. I know now that in working with God and the angels, I will always be divinely guided and protected, and if I trust my guidance and listen to them, I will be OK and will be well able to handle whatever comes my way.

One night, I had a dream about a man, and in the dream, I was given a telephone number. When I woke up, I wrote it down, and later the next day, I met a friend of mine, Kay, and told her about the dream. She was intrigued, and I showed her the number, which she recognised as the landline of an angel shop in Limerick. It was clear that Spirit was sending me a message so Kay rang the number and talked to the manager of the shop. He told me that this man was a spiritual healer and ran healing sessions there regularly.

I asked if he could put me on his appointment list. Amazingly, the person on the phone told me that somehow an appointment had already been made for me. There was no doubt that God really wanted me to meet this guy! It transpired that I was to receive not only healing from him, but he was also to become one of my mentors. I now know we learn from each other, and it turned out that I was there to help him too. As time progressed, we eventually began to work together while still being independent and in charge of our own lives.

One day, a couple of years ago, this healer said to me that he thought it was time for me to register my own business as a spiritual healer and psychic if it was going to be my full-time occupation. I thought it was a good idea, but after all I'd been through, I decided to first go to the holy well in Lixnaw to connect with Archangel Michael and see what messages I might get from him. As I sat waiting, I heard Archangel Michael say, *Go with Mary, go with Mary,* and smiled as I realised what he meant. In my work for Spirit in the future, I was to take my middle name, Mary.

That made perfect sense as I have a strong devotion to Our Blessed Lady. As soon as I confirmed that to myself, it felt right to also go with my maiden name, Madigan, because it held a legacy of many wonderful spiritual ancestors from my family. So Mary Madigan was born, which heralded a new beginning in my life.

From a childhood lived beneath the gaze of beautiful Cnoc an Óir Mountain in County Kerry to experiencing numerous trials and challenges, miracles and blessings over the years, I was now awakened to a life of service devoted to Spirit, and I understood I had a purpose.

And this is my story up to now.